Modern E
Living a Life of Excellence

Modern Bushido
Living a Life of Excellence

Bohdi Sanders, PhD

Library of Congress Cataloging-in-Publication Data
Sanders, Bohdi, 1962-
Modern Bushido: Living a Life of Excellence

ISBN – 978-1-937884-06-2

1. Martial Arts. 2. Self-Help. 3. Philosophy. I. Title

Kaizen Quest Publishing

Foreword

In 1899, Inazo Nitobe wrote the classic, *Bushido: The Warrior's Code*. He gave the early 20th Century Western world a glimpse into the mind-set of the 18th & 19th Century Samurai and the virtues of their warrior traditions. He illuminated the seven qualities of what it meant to be a Samurai, such as loyalty, integrity and respect. Drawing parallels to the knights of Europe, and their code of chivalry, he tapped into the mythical warrior archetype that lives in each of us, and more importantly, he gave us a blueprint to see how these attributes translate into everyday living.

From that blueprint, and his many years of experience as a martial artist and healer, Dr. Sanders has built a beautiful piece of work, *Modern Bushido*. Contained within these pages you are about to read, Dr. Sanders supplies you with an update of what it means to be a warrior today. Like Mr. Nitobe, yet drawing from many traditions and cultures, Dr. Sanders brings forth and illuminates the virtues and attributes that exemplify the mythical warrior that beats in the hearts of all men and women.

I have seen in my practice as a psychotherapist and helping people heal from trauma and pain, that the warrior archetype is very strong medicine indeed. The mythical warrior archetype is what empowers and connects you to the source of our own personal power. Carl Jung, the noted psycho-analyst, whose work in the identification of psychological archetypes stated, "Myth is more individual and expresses life more precisely than does science. Science works with concepts of averages which are far too general to do justice to the subjective variety of individual life."

Dr. Sanders brings to you a no watered-down version of what science or the experts tell you a warrior is or is not. He has tapped into the very essence of the Warrior's Way and brings it here to your attention today. This book is destined to become a classic in its own right. Read carefully. Digest each chapter, each page, and each sentence. Meditate upon the message. Let it sink in and feel its power. Dr. Sanders has placed it here for you to find. Be well and enjoy.

David Nelson, PhD
Martial Artist & Author of: *Black Belt Healing:*
A Martial Artist's Guide to Pain Management & Injury Recovery.

Introduction

I have studied martial arts for almost 30 years, and have seen many amazing martial artists do things with their bodies that can simply boggle the mind. I have seen some of the best fighters in the world and have trained with many martial arts instructors and other practitioners. I have also been involved in more physical confrontations than I care to remember, and know what it is like to both pound someone into a pulp, as well as be pounded. In addition, I have been trained in how to use different weapons in self-defense situations.

In short, I have witnessed and experienced a lot when it comes to the physical side of the martial arts, but with all my experience, I have found one subject that seems to always get little or no attention in the world of martial arts – how to live a life of character. Most martial arts classes are completely focused on self-defense, fighting, sport applications, tournaments, and katas. While all of these are important parts of the martial arts, there is something even more important which is missing from this list – character training.

This is what *Modern Bushido* is all about – how to live the life of the superior man. While this may sound like an elitist statement, it isn't. Living the life of the superior man is simply a way of saying living a life based on character, honor and integrity. It is living the warrior lifestyle the way it should be lived, according to universal standards and principles which make someone a superior human being.

When I say the words "superior human being," I am not referring to someone being better or more important than someone else. The phrase "superior man" was used frequently by Confucius to indicate someone who lives according to high moral standards as opposed to someone who gives little regard to such things. The superior man is not superior because he is richer, more educated, comes from a better family, or anything along those lines. He is superior because he lives his life in a superior way. He lives by higher standards than the average person.

This has always been the ideal behind the philosophy of Bushido. Literature from the 13th through the 16th centuries in Japan had many references to the ideals of Bushido. The actual word "Bushido" was first used in the 17th century, but the ideals of Bushido have been around as long as there has been a warrior class, not just in Japan, but throughout the world. Bushido did not necessarily start out as a specific set of rules that must be followed, but rather moral principles which were meant to guide the life of the warrior. More frequently than not, the principles of Bushido were simply taught to children of the warrior class from an early age as a way of life that was expected from them.

The philosophy of Bushido evolved over the centuries, but it never lost it primary focus which was living life according to the high standards expected from those of the warrior class. It is a philosophy of how to live your life as a true, complete warrior. The word "Bushido" literally means the way of the warrior. This philosophy did not limit itself to merely martial subjects. On the contrary, the philosophy of Bushido covered subjects such as how to raise children, how one should dress, how to treat your family and other people, financial issues, as well as how to conduct yourself as an honorable warrior.

Today the Bushido Code is commonly simplified to seven virtues: rectitude, courage, benevolence, respect, honesty, honor, and loyalty. But these seven virtues do not cover everything which Bushido entails; there is much more to Bushido than these seven virtues. The teachings of Bushido were meant to cover all areas of the warrior's life, not just a handful. Limiting Bushido to only these seven virtues is doing a disservice to this noble philosophy. That is where *Modern Bushido* comes into play.

In *Modern Bushido*, I discuss 30 traits which all play an important role in the warrior lifestyle. Each of these traits helps guide you in living a life of excellence. Many may question what this has to do with the life of the warrior or martial arts, but this question assumes that martial arts are merely about self-defense or fighting – they aren't. Gichin Funakoshi stated that the ultimate goal of karate is the perfection of your character, not the perfection of your martial skills.

Learning character traits, which will guide your actions throughout your life, is an important part of the martial arts, but unfortunately this is also a part that has been neglected over the years, especially in today's society where it is needed more than ever. Self-defense is merely one part of the warrior lifestyle.

The warrior lifestyle is multifaceted and entails much more than martial arts techniques. It is a complete way of life, not simply a term which encompasses anyone who practices some type of martial art. There is much more to being a true warrior than knowing how to fight. You can teach a dog to fight, but that doesn't make it a warrior.

On the contrary, the warrior lifestyle is a complete way of life. It is a way of living a life of character, honor, and integrity in every area of your life. It includes martial arts, but it is not defined by martial arts. One of the definitions of the term "warrior" is a person engaged in some struggle or conflict. The word "warrior" is not limited to someone who participates in an actual, physical battle between two armies. Many people disagree with this statement, but it is true nonetheless.

To take this definition even further, the word "war" doesn't always refer to a conflict between two countries or two groups of people. The term "war" can be defined as a struggle or competition between opposing forces or for a particular end. True warriors are not limited to those who have been in the military. Being a true warrior is dependent on how you live your life, not on what you do for a living. The true warrior is the man or woman who endeavors to live the warrior lifestyle and who lives his or her life by the code of the warrior.

And have no doubts about it, they are at war. Their struggle may not be against some opposing army, but rather it is a struggle between the opposing forces of living according to their principles of honor or living without honor. The true warrior, whether in the military or driving a garbage truck, must decide to live a life of honor and integrity according to the principles of warriorship. What you do for a living is simply what you do for a living; it is not who you are. Everyone decides for themselves whether they will live life as a true warrior or whether they will live their life in some other way.

Being a true warrior is a lifestyle, not a profession. It is not a fraternity where you have to be in the military to be considered a member. A person is a true warrior because of what is in his or her heart, mind and spirit, all the rest simply consists of the tools which the person uses to develop the warrior spirit in order to live the warrior lifestyle.

The purpose of *Modern Bushido* is to help the true warrior by being a guidebook to the tools that the warrior needs in order to develop his or her life on the path of the warrior lifestyle. This is not the final authority of the subject, but merely a guide to help you on your noble path – the path of the true warrior.

Bohdi Sanders, PhD

Modern Bushido
Living a Life of Excellence

Bohdi Sanders, PhD

Chapter 1

Character
The Nature of the Superior Man

Character: a distinctive mark; a distinctive trait, quality, or attribute; essential quality; nature; the pattern of behavior or personality found in an individual or group; moral constitution; moral or ethical strength; self-discipline.

Your character is essentially who you are as a person. It is the person that you have become through your actions and decisions over your lifetime, your essence if you will. The character of the warrior is the intrinsic qualities and principles which make him what he is – a man of integrity and honor. It is the character of the true warrior which makes him a superior man.

The true warrior, by nature and training, is indeed a superior man. He holds himself to a higher standard than most men, especially in today's society. The superior man holds his character, his reputation and the qualities which make him a man of excellence, in high esteem. To the warrior, it is his character which sets him apart from the average man. Any man can be trained to fight, but it takes much more than a set of physical skills to be a true man of honor; it takes character.

Gichin Funakoshi, the father of Shotokan karate, stated that, "The ultimate aim of Karate lies not in victory or defeat, but in the perfection of the character of the participant." The same could be said of the ultimate goal of the warrior. While it is true that the warrior trains his spirit, mind and body to be victorious when circumstances demand extraordinary action, the vast majority of the warrior's training is involved with the perfection of his character. Perfecting his character and becoming a superior man is the warrior's definitive purpose.

Furthermore, over the years, the warrior will find that he will have many more opportunities to use his character training than he will to use his physical training. Of course the warrior's physical training and the development of his character are both important parts of the warrior lifestyle, but the latter will be used on a daily basis. Every man's character is tested daily through interactions with those who he comes in contact with during his daily activities.

Therefore, it is imperative that you develop a strong moral character, and the strength to cultivate and maintain that character, once you have planted the seeds of excellence in your life. You have to decide what you stand for and what you will not stand for. Don't leave your character and your reputation to chance – take responsibility for your life. It is your duty to build your character. Nobody else will do it for you, but there are many who are willing to help you weaken it or totally destroy it.

You have to be strong enough to stand up for what you believe, even if you are standing alone. Public opinion and outside pressures should not play a part in swaying the core beliefs which make up your true character, but they will if you don't know exactly what you believe and why you believe it. You have to know why certain character traits are important to you. If your foundation is not solid, sooner or later you will find problems which are a direct result of your shaky foundation.

Your character is the foundation of all the other parts of the warrior lifestyle. Without a solid foundation, it is easy for you to veer off track in one way or another. For this reason, it is vital that your character adheres to the highest standards. Don't compromise where your character is concerned. This is just one of the traits that sets the warrior apart as a superior man. Work to build a solid character and maintain a reputation which is true to your nature as a superior man.

This brings us to the question of how do you compose your character. How does a person develop a set of qualities or traits in his life that sets him apart from the common man? Where do you start? This can be an especially tricky question if one does not have background knowledge concerning what comprises good character traits, or if one has failed to live a life filled with these positive qualities over the years.

The best way to start to compose your character or to change your character if need be, is to study the traits which you want to incorporate into your life. Study the traits of the superior men of the past. What made these men "men of character?" Why do you admire decision, there will be times when things do not go as you would like them to. The point is that you must have the personal integrity to make those decisions from a mindset of "what is right."

To continue with my example, the man of integrity would never lie for purely financial profit or to take advantage of some innocent victim. He chooses his actions according to what is right, and that would clearly be wrong. Men of integrity impose certain restrictions on themselves. This is where their principles come into play. The character traits in this book are presented as guidance for you to develop your own personal set of principles by which to live, but each one must be tempered by the dictates of right and wrong in any given situation.

This takes personal integrity. No one is going to force you to develop these character traits. No one is going to force you to live up to the principles by which you have decided to live. If you do not have the personal integrity to follow through and live up to your own personal code, then that is your choice. You have the right to live your life as you see fit, as long as it does not interfere with others doing the same.

It is solely on your shoulders to develop your character and your personal integrity. This is what the warrior lifestyle is all about – disciplining yourself and having the integrity to live a life of excellence. You are the captain of this ship. It is up to you!

Dr. Charles Hackney, in his excellent book, *Martial Virtues*, states, "Integrity may be considered a form of justice-turned-inward in which, rather than an honorable persona demanding to be treated in a certain manner, the honorable person behaves in a manner that is true to his ideals...Rather than honor being found in conforming to others' expectations, honor is found by living up to one's own beliefs and internalized stands of right and wrong."

Having personal integrity does not mean living up to the expectations of others. It means having the self-discipline to live your life according to your own standards of right and wrong. The catch here is that your standards of right and wrong must be derived from the correct principles that guide men of integrity. If everyone on this planet decided for themselves what is right and wrong, we would have chaos.

The difference in everyone deciding for themselves what is right and what is wrong, is that the man of principle makes his decision from a place of honor and integrity. His conscience is highly developed to the point of internally understanding what is right and what is wrong. He holds himself to a much higher standard than other people. As Emerson said, "What I must do is all that concerns me, not what the people think."

Lao Tzu said the same thing but in a slightly different way stating, "Highly evolved people have their own conscience as pure law." For the man of integrity, living life according to what you believe to be right and wrong is not a license to do whatever you may want to do. Rather it means that you put what is right over all other considerations. But, to do so, you must first develop yourself to a point of internally knowing what is right and what is wrong.

In addition, personal integrity means that you will also have to be willing to accept the consequences of your decisions. Doing what you know is right will not exempt you from the consequences of governmental laws, but the man of integrity will do what is right nonetheless because he answers to his own conscience first and foremost. Moliere, the famous French playwright, put it this way, "It is not only what we do, but what we do not do, for which we are accountable."

The person of integrity can be trusted to do what is right because he answers first and foremost to his conscience. He does not look to others to justify his actions. He makes his decisions according to the firm, but not rigid, principles by which he lives. It is this dedication to his principles that enables him to live a life of excellence and which sets him above the common man.

Without personal integrity, it would be impossible to truly live the warrior lifestyle. You will find as you continue to read *Modern Bushido*, that the warrior lifestyle is not a passive lifestyle. It takes dedication and hard work. It takes self-discipline and perseverance. There will be many times when it would be easier for you to relax your standards and let some of your principles slide, times when no one would know but yourself.

The only thing that will keep you on track during times like that is your personal integrity and dedication to the principles that you have made a firm decision to live by on your journey to live the warrior lifestyle. Thomas Jefferson explained how he dealt with such situations stating, "Whenever you are to do a thing, though it can never be known but to yourself, ask yourself how you would act were all the world looking at you, and act accordingly."

Living with integrity has to be a 24/7 process, even when you are alone. To do right only when others are watching or listening, and live another way when you are alone, is merely being hypocritical.

continually dwell on day in and day out. If you do not want something to manifest in your life, don't allow your mind to dwell on it.

Wayne Dyer teaches that, "Every thought you have can be assessed in terms of whether it strengthens or weakens you." This is something else that science is proving. Your thoughts can directly affect your body. Martial artists know that their thoughts play a big part in what they can accomplish in the arts. If you think that you can't do a kick or that you can't defeat a certain opponent, your mind and body will respond to that thought. If you doubt this, test it out in the weight room. See if you can feel a difference in your weight training between days when your mind is focused and days when it is preoccupied with outside thoughts.

Bodybuilders know how important a focused mind is to their overall training results. Arnold Schwarzenegger wrote in his comprehensive bodybuilding book, *The Encyclopedia of Modern Bodybuilding*, "The body will never fully respond to your workouts until you understand how to train the mind as well. The mind is a dynamo, a source of vital energy. That energy can be negative and work against you, or you can harness it to give yourself unbelievable workouts and build a physique that lives up to your wildest expectations." Schwarzenegger went on to say, "When the going gets tough, it is always the mind that fails first, not the body."

It is important for the warrior to keep his mind focused on the things which strengthen him rather than weaken him. Maintain your mental balance and don't let the daily aggravations and stresses unbalance your mind. Negative, stressful thoughts weaken you, while positive thoughts strengthen you. You can look at your thoughts as your inner pep talk. This inner conversation with yourself can make you powerful or weak, happy or unhappy, confident or unconfident. Never forget that your thoughts are powerful forces.

As with all powerful forces, they can be used either to help you or used against you. The good news is that when it comes to your thoughts, you are the only person who is in control. Thus it is you who makes the decision concerning whether your thoughts will strengthen you and move you towards your goals, or whether they will work against you and weaken you.

Thoughts of anger, hate, resentment, revenge, and unforgiveness, which most likely include all of the other four emotions, are all thoughts which will weaken you and work against you. Although I do not have room to go into the subject of unforgiveness in this chapter, it is a subject that would serve you well to do some reading on if you find that this is an area that you have a problem with in your life. Unforgiveness can be like a hidden pool of quicksand on the path of the warrior lifestyle; once you step into it, you are basically stuck in that spot until you get out of it and leave it behind you.

I mentioned earlier that ultimately it is your thoughts that make you honorable or dishonorable. It is the intention behind your actions which determine if your actions are honorable or dishonorable, and your intention comes from your thoughts. An action which seems right to outside observers, but which originates from dishonorable intentions, is not an honorable action, even if there is nothing inherently wrong with the action itself. This can be a little hard for most people to grasp, but it is very important to true warriors who take their honor seriously.

In order for an action to truly be good or right, the thought behind it must be right. In essence, things have to be right on the inside for them to truly be right on the outside. You can't do wrong right, but you can do right wrong. The intention behind your action makes all the difference in the world. People may judge you on the outcome, but your honor does not depend on the outcome, it depends on the intention behind your action.

If your mind is right and your intentions are honorable, you can rest easy knowing that you have acted honorably, no matter what happens. A conscience free from guilt leads to tranquility of the mind, and only a tranquil mind can see things as they truly are. This is one of the benefits of meditation. By quieting the mind through meditation, you are better able to think rationally and clear the fog that can sometimes cloud the mind. Not only should the warrior learn to meditate as part of his quest to learn to control his mind, but he should also meditate on what he wants to manifest in his life through his thought processes.

The important thing to understand from this chapter is that your thoughts are extremely important. They play a major part in either the success or the failure of everything that you do. You can literally change your world by changing your thoughts. Napoleon Hill wrote, "We are the master of our fate, the captains of our souls, because we have the power to control our thoughts." There are many things outside of the realm of your control, but your thoughts are one thing that you have total control over. You dictate your path by controlling your thoughts.

Meditations on Correct Thought

Human beings, by changing the inner attitudes of their
minds, can change the outer aspects of their lives.
William James

We are what we think. All that we are arises with
our thoughts. With our thoughts, we make the world.
Buddha

Understand that what you think about expands.
Wayne Dyer

The superior man is committed to focus.
Hsun Tzu

When we direct our thoughts properly,
we can control our emotions.
W. Clement Stone

Only in quiet waters things mirror
themselves undistorted. Only in a quiet
mind is adequate perception of the world.
Margolis

Your thoughts create your reality because your thoughts
determine how you respond to situations in your daily life.
Wayne Dyer

What the mind of man can conceive and believe,
the mind of a man can achieve.
Napoleon Hill

Think like a man of action, act like a man of thought.
Thomas Mann

The things you think about determine the quality of your
mind. Your soul takes on the color of your thoughts.
Marcus Aurelius

Whatever you think, be sure it is what you think.
T. S. Eliot

Be careful of your thoughts;
they are the beginning of your acts.
Lao Tzu

To return, time after time,
to the same annoyance,
is a sort of insanity.
Baltasar Gracian

Deliberate often – decide once.
Latin proverb

The whole dignity of man is in thought.
Labor then to think right.
Pascal

Change your thoughts, and you change your world.
Norman Vincent Peale

Chapter 5

Right Actions
The Warrior's Building Blocks

Action: The doing of something; behavior; habitual conduct; habitual activity characterized by energy and boldness

Emerson stated that, "A man's action is only a picture book of his creed." Your actions do indeed show to the world who you truly are as a person, and what your inner beliefs and philosophy are. Your behavior is constantly revealing something about you to those whom you interact with throughout your life. As F. D. Huntington said, "What a man does, tells us what he is." For this reason, it is vitally important to think before you act and carefully consider all of your actions.

The philosophy that your actions reveal the true you, has been taught throughout the ages from some of the earliest wisdom teachings right up to the present day. Ptah-Hotep taught this, as did Jesus and Lao Tzu. The fact that men of honor should carefully consider their actions and act appropriately, according to their own code of honor, is universally accepted, but seems to be taken less than seriously, especially in today's society. Although most people don't seem to take their actions seriously anymore, the warrior doesn't live like most people. He knows how important it is to carefully consider his every action.

As I discussed in the last chapter, your actions begin with your thoughts, so it is vital that you control your mind and your emotions or you will never be able to control your actions. If you allow your mind to run wild, entertaining any and every thought that pops into your head, then your actions will follow along, and you will find that you are randomly doing whatever, without giving your actions much thought at all.

The same goes for allowing your emotions to control your actions. The man who acts according to his emotions, instead of giving his actions rational thought, will find that he is constantly behaving in ways which are contrary to who he truly wants to be. Allowing emotions such as fear, anger, frustration, hate, envy, or jealousy to control your actions is only asking for trouble, and will damage your reputation and disrupt your goals on your quest to become a true warrior. You must take steps to control both your thoughts and your emotions in order to ensure that your actions are right.

This is the first step toward acting correctly in every circumstance. You must get your mind right before you can possibly make your actions right. As Ashley Montagu pointed out, "The only measure of what you believe is what you do. If you want to know what people believe, don't read what they write, don't ask what they believe, just observe what they do." Actions originate from your thoughts, so learning to control your thoughts and thinking rationally, instead of emotionally, is the foundation of right actions.

Others can see what you truly believe by how you act. Jesus taught, "You will know them by their fruits." John Locke echoed this thought saying, "The actions of men are the best interpreters of their thoughts." It is easy for someone to profess to believe in a certain philosophy, but it is their actions which serve as proof of either what they truly believe, or how seriously they believe what they espouse.

The true warrior should walk the walk, not merely talk the talk. It is easy to say you believe in the virtues and traits of the warrior lifestyle, but it takes more than a verbal pronouncement of these virtues to actually live the lifestyle; you have to make these virtues and traits an active part of your life. In short, your actions have to coincide with your professed beliefs. There is an old Chinese proverb which states, "To talk good is not to be good; to do good, that is being good." This is very true.

The warrior's words will correspond with his actions, and his actions will correspond with his words. Lao Tzu taught, "The Universal Way is not just a matter of speaking wisdom, but one of continual practice." This could also be said of living the warrior lifestyle. It is not a matter of talking about all the things which make the warrior lifestyle a great way to live, you actually have to live it – practice it.

You don't live the warrior lifestyle to impress others; you live the warrior lifestyle because of a personal decision to live a life of excellence. You don't do the right thing for any kind of personal reward or to impress those around you; you do the right thing simply because it is right. The warrior does what he knows is right according to his own code of honor, without worrying about what others think about it. He knows that he alone is responsible for his actions, no one else.

The *Hadith* states, "Do what you should do when you should do it; don't do what you shouldn't do; and when it is unclear, wait until you are more sure." This is good advice for the warrior. Although this is pretty simple and straightforward advice, it is not always so simple to figure out what you should do and what you shouldn't do. Again, this requires thought, and to make the right decisions, you have to spend time making sure your mind is right. Remember, for things to be right on the outside, they first have to be right on the inside. If you aren't thinking rationally, there is a very good chance that your decisions will be off kilter.

Thinking before you act is not enough, you must think rationally and correctly before you act. Misguided, emotional thoughts will lead to bad decisions and bad actions. Marcus Aurelius taught that you should, "Say and do everything according to the soundest reason." This is another maxim which is universally taught throughout the world.

So, what should you do if you really do not know what to do in a certain situation? Wait and meditate until you do know what you should do. Bodhidharma, the 6th century Buddhist monk and Zen patriarch, stated, "If you're not sure, don't act." This is good advice for the warrior. You don't have to make a snap decision. Wait until you know what the right action is in your spirit, then act. Pythagoras stated you should, "Consult and deliberate before you act, that you may not commit foolish actions."

Of course there will be times when you do not have the luxury of meditating on what you should do before you make a decision. It is because of this that you should be doing daily meditation and studying in order to be able to make the right decision when you find yourself in a situation which requires you to act immediately. You have to be prepared ahead of time to make the right decision in these instances.

How do you do this? How do you ensure that you will be prepared to make the right decision when you do not have time to spend hours or days determining the right move? You make the virtues and traits of the warrior lifestyle a part of you through constant study and integration of them in your life. By understanding what you stand for and what you know is right, you are much better prepared to deal with life's curve balls when they are thrown at you.

You wouldn't wait until some mugger attacks you, before you start preparing to defend yourself. That would be silly. Martial artists spend years training and learning the art of self-defense in order to be prepared, should they ever need to use their skills. The same goes for your decision making skills. You have to study and prepare your mind to make the right decision *before* you are face to face with an important choice. Study the teachings of the wise men from throughout history. My book, *Wisdom of the Elders*, is an excellent aid to help you prepare your mind to make the right decisions throughout life.

Another factor that determines whether your actions are right or wrong is the intention behind your actions. Your intentions should be sincere and pure. Sheikh Muzaffer stated, "The first duty is to behave with purity of intention. It should never be forgotten that every deed and every action is judged according to the intention behind it."

This doesn't mean that you need to disclose your intentions or your motives to everyone else; that is not always a wise decision. What it does mean is that you should be making your decisions based on what is right and what is wrong. La Rochefoucauld, in his great book, *Maxims*, wrote, "We should often blush at our noblest deeds if the world were to see all their underlying motives." This should never be said of the true warrior.

The warrior's motives should be based on honor and doing what is right. Although you don't always want to disclose the motives behind your actions, ideally, you should never be ashamed of those motives because they will come from a place of honor and integrity. Many times, people will not understand your actions, but this is not your problem. La Rochefoucauld went on to write, "A countless number of acts that appear foolish have secret motives that are very wise and weighty."

Your objective is not for everyone to understand your actions, or the intentions behind your actions, only that your actions are honorable and right. People will read what they will into your actions. To quote La Rochefoucauld again, "Our actions are like rhymes: anyone can fit them in to mean what he likes." People will believe what they want to believe. What someone else thinks or believes about your actions shouldn't concern you. Remember what Marcus Aurelius wrote, "It is quite possible to be a good man without anyone realizing it…I do what is mine to do; the rest doesn't disturb me."

Concern yourself more with what is right, have the courage to act on what you know is right, and leave others to believe what they will. Focus on your own actions, not the actions of others. Yes, there will be times when you have to respond to what others do, but when you do respond, always do so from the standpoint of what is right. As Takuan Soho taught, "Each action of the warrior is performed from a place of fundamental wisdom...it is completely different from the ordinary behavior of a fool. Even if it looks the same, it is different on the inside."

How can an action look the same as what some unthinking, moron does and yet not be the same? The answer is because it is different on the inside. This means that it comes from a place of honor and integrity. It doesn't matter what it looks like to others, it matters what the intention is behind the action. Remember this and make sure your intentions are always honorable and originate from a place of integrity.

To do this, you must first understand your objectives and your motivations. Marshall Ferdinand Foch stated, "In whatever position you find yourself determine first your objective." Guan Yin Tzu also taught this reasoning stating, "The secret of success is before attempting anything, be very clear about why you are doing it." If you don't know your objective or the purpose behind your action, how can you possibly know if your actions are right? You must know why you are doing what you are doing, and what you want to accomplish with your actions. Your objective determines your actions.

Why are you learning martial arts? Why do you spend hours each week practicing self-defense? Why do you want to live the warrior lifestyle? Why is meditating important to you? These are all important questions for you to ask yourself. It is vitally important for you to be clear on why you do what you do. If you don't have a clear picture of what you want, and you don't really understand why it is important for you to continue to work to achieve your goals, you will find that it will be much harder to keep yourself motivated.

Having a deep understanding, concerning why you are doing what you do, is vital to keeping yourself on track. This is like having a roadmap that guides you to where you want to go, and this roadmap also helps guide you concerning what you should and should not do. There are certain actions which will bring you closer to your goals and other actions which will take you further away from your goals. Keeping your mind focused on what is important to you helps you determine which actions are which.

In addition to knowing what you should and should not do, you also want to pay attention to how you perform your deeds. Swami Sivananda taught that you should, "Put your heart, mind, intellect, and soul even to your smallest acts. This is the secret to success." Multi-tasking may be a part of life today, but it is not the best way to get things done, especially if you are interested in excellence. There is a Zen maxim that states, "When walking, walk. When eating, eat." This means that you should focus on the task at hand. Whatever you are doing, do it to the best of your ability – do it well.

The warrior puts his whole heart into his actions whether he is working out or planting a garden. He is a man of excellence and this should be evident in his every action. Do one thing at a time, do it well, then focus on something else. I like what John W. Gardner wrote, "Do ordinary things extraordinarily well." This quote is one that every warrior should meditate on and keep in mind.

Confucius taught, "By nature, men are nearly alike; by practice, they get to be wide apart." It is your actions which set you apart from ordinary men and make you a superior man. Anne Byrhhe wrote, "Every action we take, everything we do, is either a victory or defeat in the struggle to become what we want to be." Your actions matter. You have to start from where you are and begin to transform your actions (if your actions haven't been what they should be). Lao Tzu wrote, "A journey of a thousand miles begins with one step."

It doesn't matter what you have done in the past; you can always start anew where your actions are concerned. Start to act like the man of honor that you want to be, today. Always remember, everything you do, everything you think, and everything you say, has some consequence in your life, or the lives of others. You can do wrong, not only by your actions, but by your inactions, and you are responsible for both. Moliere wrote, "It is not only what we do, but also what we do not do, for which we are accountable."

Doing nothing is also an action; not making a decision is making a decision. Everything you do is an action, even if it is the action of inaction. By deciding not to workout, but instead to take the afternoon off and sit in front of the television, you are still acting. Watching television is an action. Taking a nap is an action. Everything that you do is some type of action. Whenever you decide not to do one thing, you are deciding to do something else. This is true even if what you decide to do is *nothing*. Doing *nothing* is in fact doing *something*.

What the warrior should always be concerned with is whether his actions are right or wrong. Always use your sense of honor to determine the correct course of action, and remember, as Plutarch pointed out, "Not even the gods can undo what has been done." You can't go back and change the past; all you can do is start to do right, right now, this very moment. Starting now, strive to make your every action right, according to your own code of honor.

Meditations on Right Actions

First say to yourself what you would be;
and then do what you have to do.
Epictetus

Every man is the sum of his own works.
Cervantes

If the heart is right the deeds will be right.
Japanese Proverb

Let your words correspond with your
actions and your actions with your words.
Confucius

A man's action is only a picture book of his creed.
Emerson

Every action we take, everything we do, is either a victory
or defeat in the struggle to become what we want to be.
Anne Byrhhe

When walking, walk. When eating, eat.
Zen Maxim

A journey of a thousand miles begins with one step.
Lao Tzu

Our grand business is not to see what lies dimly at
a distance, but to do what lies clearly at hand.
Thomas Carlyle

The success of very important matters often depends on
doing or not doing something that seems trivial. Even in
little things, therefore, you must be cautious and thoughtful.
Francesco Guicciardini

Never refuse or hesitate to take steps against
impending dangers...because you think they are too late.
Since things often take much longer than expected,
because of their very nature and because of the various
obstacles they encounter, it very often happens that the
steps you have omitted to take, thinking they would have
been too late, would have been in time.
Francesco Guicciardini

We should often blush at our noblest deeds if
the world were to see all their underlying motives.
La Rochefoucauld

Consult and deliberate before you act,
that you may not commit foolish actions.
Pythagoras

It is not only what we do, but also what we
do not do, for which we are accountable.
Moliere

Chapter 6

Correct Speech
The Words of the Warrior

Speech: the act of speaking; expression or communication of thoughts and feelings by spoken words; the manner of speaking; that which is spoken; utterance, remark, statement, talk, conversation.

Your speech is how you communicate with others. It is how you allow others to know your feelings and thoughts. In essence, your speech, along with your actions, is the only way that other people can judge you and your character. For this reason, among others, it is very important that you keep a close watch over what you say and how you say it. Yes, how you express yourself can be just as important as what you say. Your attitude and tone can tell someone as much about what you are communicating as your actual words. As the Viking book of wisdom, *The Havamal*, states, "Man by his speech is known to men."

After your actions, your speech is the most important factor in how people see you as a person. This is why it is important for the warrior to take some time to *think* about the way he wants his speech to portray him as a man of character, the pitfalls to be aware of, and the factors which can help ensure that his speech is an asset instead of a liability in his quest to perfect himself on his journey to become a superior man. The key part of that last sentence is the word "think."

Always think *before* you speak. The Buddhist philosopher, Nagarjuna, stated, "Those who speak with discretion are respected by mankind." So according to Nagarjuna, discretion in your speech is the key to being respected by others. This means that you have to give some thought to your words *before* you allow them to come out of your mouth. Think about what you are going to say, how it will be received by those who are listening to you, even those that you may not be aware are listening, and your purpose in speaking, all before you start talking.

It is not necessary or advantageous to give your opinion about everything to everyone. It is not your job to be a form of cheap entertainment for those around you. This is a trap that is very easy to fall into and is the downfall of many people. While it is certainly okay to chat with your buddies or other people about meaningless things in order to be affable, you should be careful of your conversation even on such relaxed occasions. It is all too easy to get carried away with your conversation and express opinions which can be offensive and used against you at a later time. Be genial and social, but at the same time be aware and thoughtful concerning your private beliefs.

Even if you are talking to people who you consider harmless and well-intentioned, you never know how your words will be taken or to whom they will be repeated. It is always good policy to carefully monitor your speech, even when chatting with friends. Francesco Guicciardini stated, "Unless you are forced by necessity, be careful in your conversations never to say anything which, if repeated, might displease others. For often, at times and in ways you could never foresee, those words may do you great harm. In this matter, I warn you, be very careful. Even prudent men go wrong here, and it is difficult not to."

Confucius also taught the importance of watching what you say. He pointed out, "For one word a man is often deemed to be wise, and for one word he is often deemed to be foolish. We should be careful indeed of what we say." You will notice that neither Confucius nor Guicciardini made an exception concerning when you are talking to friends or enemies, or when you are talking in private or in public. They simply warned us to be very careful when it comes to your speech.

If you will remember, I wrote that it is not only your words which are important, but also your tone and how you speak, that should be taken into account. Speech is simply how you communicate with others, and there is much more that goes into this communication than simple words. Meanings can be communicated through other means as well, such as gestures, tone, and the overall way that you say what you are saying.

Someone can say something to you such as, "How nice for you," and it can mean something other than he is happy for you, depending on how he says it. A sarcastic tone could indicate that he is jealous of you or is upset with you, whereas, if it is stated in a sincere manner, it probably means exactly what the words state. How you say something is just as important as what you say, or at least fairly close. John

Wayne gave some good advice concerning this when he said, "Talk low, talk slow, and don't say too much."

Ben Johnson stated that, "Talking and eloquence are not the same: to speak, and to speak well, are two different things. A fool may talk, but a wise man speaks." You do not have to be loud and obnoxious to get your point across. In fact, speaking in a loud, angry tone, while sometimes necessary, is not the way to win over most people or to leave someone with a favorable impression of yourself. Learn to use soft words, backed up with rational, hard arguments. Nagarjuna taught, "The steadfast who speak in few words and politely are very much respected by mankind."

There is a time and a place for different kinds of speech, but there is never a time or a place for thoughtless speech. Always think before you speak, no matter what the situation may be. The trick is to watch and listen to your audience before you start speaking. Judge the nature, character, and beliefs of those around you before you speak, then you are better able to speak without stepping on their toes or making any comments which they may find offensive and which may come back to cause you some grief at a later time.

Benjamin Franklin said, "Would you persuade, speak of interest, not of reason." Don't expect everyone to understand things as well as you or to think rationally. Not everyone is rational or has the capability to understand the warrior lifestyle and how you live your life, but you can still carry on a nice, social conversation with them by speaking in terms of things that they are interested in and allowing them to do most of the talking. You don't have to try to show everyone the error of their ways. Not only is this unwanted by the vast majority of people, but it hardly ever works, and most people simply find that offensive. You have to be smart and realize that not everyone thinks like you.

It is best to not speak about yourself. Get others to talk about themselves instead. People love to talk about themselves and their lives. Nobody likes to talk to someone who is obsessed with his own life and goes on and on about every detail of his "all-important" life, with little or no interest in anybody or anything else. The key to being a good conversationalist is to know how to get people talking about things which interest them.

There are several advantages in doing this. First, the other person will like talking to you and will consider you a great conversationalist, even without you saying much. Also, you are able to learn much more about someone when they are talking and sharing things, as opposed to you doing so. It is always to your advantage to listen and learn instead of talking, but this takes discipline and practice. It is human nature to want to add your two cents to the conversation. Resist this urge unless there is some purpose in your adding to the discourse.

Taisou taught, "One offensive word is enough to leave a permanent scar that may become a seed for revenge." It is so easy to allow your emotions to get involved during a conversation and to permit yourself to vent your anger or frustrations through your words. While this feels really good at the time, later it can come back to cause you many problems. It is just not worth the risk or the stress of wondering if what you said will be used against you in some way. When you resist the urge to spout off and express your opinion, you are guaranteed not to have to deal with any adverse consequences of your speech at a later time. As the Talmud teaches, "Your friend has a friend, and your friend's friend has a friend; be discreet."

Even if you are speaking to someone who you consider close, it is wise to watch what you say because it may be repeated or used against you somewhere down the road, when your relationship may not be as close. Samuel Johnson explained the reason behind this well when he wrote, "A man should be careful never to tell tales of himself to his own disadvantage; people may be amused, and laugh at the time, but they will be remembered, and brought up against him upon some subsequent occasion."

Relationships change, just like everything else in this world. Someone you may be on friendly terms with today may change his feelings towards you in the future and use things you have disclosed to him against you. It is the safest policy not to disclose personal information which can be used against you and to carefully watch what you say. Don't allow yourself to get carried away during any conversation.

This is especially important when you are highly emotional or angry. Always be extremely careful and mindful of your words when you are angry. During periods of anger, your mind will scream at you that, "It doesn't care about the consequences; you should put this person in his place." It is during times like this that you have to take control of your emotions, and your urge to let someone know exactly how you feel, and think rationally before you speak. Never allow your negative emotions to control your tongue. Harsh words, combined with poor reasoning, never settle anything; they only make things worse.

By being a man of few words and controlling your speech, you will be better assured of not being thoughtless in your speech. La

Rochefoucauld wrote, "As the stamp of great minds is to suggest much in few words, so, contrariwise, little minds have the gift of talking a great deal and saying nothing." You want to conduct yourself as someone with a great mind, whose words have meaning, not be seen as someone who continually chatters and says nothing, or whose words are meaningless and should be taken with a grain of salt.

The warrior will carefully consider his speech, not simply to keep himself out of trouble, but because his speech is a part of his character. It is best for the warrior to be more introspective. He should communicate more with himself than with others, focusing on making himself the best he can be, instead of being interested in the latest gossip. Confucius taught, "A superior man is modest in his speech, but exceeds in his actions." This should be the goal of the warrior where speech is concerned. Be modest and sincere in your speech and make sure your actions coincide with what you say.

The fundamental nature of the warrior is to say what you mean and mean what you say. In order to do this, you have to be careful concerning what you say. Never promise to do something if you don't plan on doing it or cannot fulfill your promise. Shakespeare pointed out that, "Things are often spoke and seldom meant." This is the way of the average man, but should not be the way of the warrior. When the warrior says something, he means it and backs it up with his actions.

It is for this reason that he has to be careful not to say that he will do something simply to please the person he is talking to. Don't say you will do something then put it out of your mind as if you never mentioned it. That is merely a way to destroy your reputation as a man of character with those around you. You want to be known as a man of your word, a man whose word is as good as gold, not someone who simply spouts off and doesn't mean what he says. People will take notice of this and will not take you seriously if you say things and never back them up.

The same principle goes for exaggerating. When you relay a story or tell someone what you have witnessed, don't exaggerate. Baltasar Gracian explained exactly why you should not exaggerate, stating, "Never exaggerate...avoid offending the truth, in part to avoid the cheapening of your judgment. Exaggeration wastes distinction, and testifies to the paucity of your understanding." Essentially, when you exaggerate you are either lying to make your words seem more important, or you are giving evidence that your judgment is not to be trusted. Neither of these should be characteristics of the true warrior.

To avoid this, it is best to not talk about things which you are not sure about. Always remember that your ignorance exceeds your knowledge. Don't try to seem smarter or better informed than you are by talking about things which you don't understand or on which you don't have complete information. As Syrus taught, "Keep the golden mean between saying too much and saying too little." Trying to impress people by attempting to appear better informed or better educated than you actually are, will usually come back to embarrass you, as there is always someone out there who is better informed or better educated than you on different subjects.

Instead of trying to impress people, simply be sincere and be yourself. If you do not know something, keep your mouth shut, listen, and learn. Abraham Lincoln stated this principle perfectly when he said, "It is better to keep one's mouth shut and be thought a fool than to open it and resolve all doubt." Speaking about things which you don't understand, as though you are an expert on the subject, is a characteristic of a fool, not a characteristic of the warrior.

C. J. Ducasse said, "To speak of *mere words* is much like speaking of *mere dynamite*." By now you should be starting to understand how important your speech and words are, and why you should take pains to think carefully before you speak. Swami Shivananda stated that, "He who has control over his tongue is greater than a hero in battle." What he meant by this statement is that it is extremely hard to perfect the trait of controlling your tongue. It is human nature to like to talk, to brag, and to freely communicate one's thoughts, but it is not human nature to take control and carefully monitor your speech.

When in doubt about what to say, say nothing. Aesop stated, "In dangerous times wise men say nothing." This is always the safest policy when you are unsure what to say – simply remain silent. There are many times when silence says much more than words can convey. You are not obligated to respond to everyone simply because they would like you to. Many times people try to set you up to say something that they can use against you. By remaining silent, you both spoil their little trap and maintain your dignity and peace of mind.

Don't let your tongue be your own worst enemy; learn to control your emotions and your speech. It is always best to keep your private information secret. Don't be too open or too eager to share your personal thoughts. There is a time for speech and a time for silence, and it is wisdom to know when it is time to speak and when it is time to remain silent. I will end this chapter with some wisdom from a Latin proverb, "From a little spark may burst a mighty flame."

Meditations on Correct Speech

If the bird hadn't sung, it wouldn't have been shot.
Japanese Proverb

Keep the golden mean between saying
too much and saying too little.
Syrus

In times like these men should utter nothing for
which they would not be willingly responsible
through time and in eternity.
Abraham Lincoln

You always win by not saying
the things you don't need to say.
Chinese Proverb

A superior man is modest in his speech,
but exceeds in his actions.
Confucius

Say but little, and say it well.
Irish Proverb

Eloquence resides no less in a person's tone of voice,
expression, and general bearing than in his choice of words.
La Rochefoucauld

Of what does not concern you say nothing good or bad.
Italian Proverb

In dangerous times wise men say nothing.
Aesop

A gentle response allays wrath;
A harsh word provokes anger.
The Book of Proverbs

Think before you speak but do not speak all that you think.
Chinese Proverb

Both speech and silence transgress.
Zen Maxim

Unless you are forced by necessity, be careful in your
conversations never to say anything which, if repeated,
might displease others. For often, at times and in ways you
could never foresee, those words may do you great harm.
Francesco Guicciardini

Judge the nature of your listeners and speak accordingly.
Tiruvalluvar

Outside noisy, inside empty.
Chinese Proverb

You cannot talk to a frog in a well about the vast sea;
he is limited to his area of space.
A summer insect has no knowledge of snow;
it knows nothing beyond its own season.
Chiu Shu

Chapter 7

Wisdom
The Way of the Sage

Wisdom: the quality of being wise; power of judging rightly and following the soundest course of action, based on knowledge, experience, understanding; good judgment; sagacity.

Wisdom is the quality of being wise. That is a pretty simplistic definition and is not very helpful in understanding why wisdom is important to the warrior, but if you read the other definitions, you begin to understand why wisdom is so important to the warrior lifestyle. Wisdom enables the warrior to judge rightly and to follow the soundest course of action based on knowledge and understanding. This encompasses exactly what the warrior needs in order to live the warrior lifestyle in a world where good judgment is becoming a rarity.

The Roman philosopher, Cicero, agreed with the current definition of wisdom, stating, "The function of wisdom is to discriminate between good and evil." Thoreau wrote that, "It is a characteristic of wisdom not to do desperate things." Both of these require understanding and good judgment, which is exactly what wisdom provides for you. Without wisdom you are basically shooting in the dark. It is vital for the warrior that he strives to obtain wisdom and puts that wisdom to use in his life.

Buddha called wisdom the most precious of riches. The book of *Proverbs* says, "Get wisdom, get understanding...Do not forsake wisdom, and she will protect you; love her, and she will watch over you. Wisdom is supreme; therefore get wisdom." This is good advice, but exactly how does one become a wise man with a store of wisdom to guide him throughout his life?

Like most things, which are valuable and worthwhile, wisdom requires effort and work. Just as the fruit tree doesn't produce fruit overnight, you can't sit down with a book one day and think that you will have obtained wisdom the next day. Actually, I guess you could read a book one day and *think* that you have obtained wisdom the next day, but thinking that you are wise and being wise are two different things. None of the traits found in *Modern Bushido* are developed overnight; they all take discipline and the hand of time to develop. The development of wisdom is no different.

So let's get back to the question about how one obtains wisdom. If you look back at the definition of wisdom, you will notice that it is based on knowledge, experience and understanding. Knowledge is learning and can come from anyone or anything. Always be open to learning from everything you read, everyone you meet, and everything you do. Lord Chesterfield wrote, "There is hardly any place or any company where you may not gain knowledge, if you please; almost everybody knows some one thing, and is glad to talk about that one thing."

Baltasar Gracian stated, "A man without knowledge, a world in darkness." Knowledge is the beginning of wisdom. Without some knowledge of how things work in this world, it is impossible to have any understanding of how the world works, and therefore impossible to develop wisdom. Sakya Pandit put it plainly when he said, "Of what use is a man who has acquired little knowledge?"

The first step in developing wisdom is to become knowledgeable. Study and learn about many different subjects, but especially about the subjects that can affect your life and the lives of your loved ones. For the warrior, developing a vast array of knowledge is crucial, especially knowledge that guides him on his journey through the warrior lifestyle. To be a superior man, you must acquire as much knowledge as you possibly can. Never stop learning.

Ramakrishna, the famous Indian mystic, stated, "He alone is truly a man who is illuminated by the light of the true knowledge." You must obtain true knowledge, not simply a bunch of facts which you file away in your memory bank. Being able to recite hundreds of facts and figures does you little good, unless you make a living on game shows. You have to be able to put the knowledge which you acquire to use for it to be valuable in your life. This is where understanding comes into play.

Understanding is the ability to truly comprehend or grasp the principles behind the subject which you are learning. In essence, it is being able to put your knowledge to work. It is this intellectual capacity to truly understand what you learn that makes it useful.

Without a true understanding of something, it is difficult to really benefit from it.

Of course there are exceptions to this statement. You don't have to have a deep understanding of how your refrigerator works in order to put a bottle of water in it and keep it cold. But if your refrigerator quits working, you have to have a thorough understanding of how it works in order to fix it. Only the man who has acquired that knowledge, and knows how to put that knowledge to work, can successfully use his understanding to fix the unexpected problem of his refrigerator not working correctly. This applies to everything in life. You can get by with a little knowledge, but sooner or later, knowledge without understanding will catch up with you and reveal your deficiency.

This same principle can be applied to your martial arts training. If you simply memorize certain kicks or punches, that is basic knowledge. But in order to successfully use those kicks or punches, you need to thoroughly understand the underlying principles behind them. You need to know more than merely how to throw a punch or kick in the air. A true understanding of the usefulness of the punch or kick would entail knowing where to place it on your attacker's body to stop him, how it feels to strike an actual person, an understanding of the human anatomy, etc.

As you can plainly see, acquiring a deep understanding of a subject involves much more than a rudimentary knowledge of the subject; it goes much deeper and gets down to the actual principles behind the knowledge. To achieve a genuine comprehension of something, you have to completely understand how and why it works. This applies to everything you do, whether it is gardening or martial arts. And, to completely understand something, your knowledge has to come from experience. You can't *completely* understand anything by simply reading about it or hearing about it from someone else – you have to experience it for yourself.

Experience is the third part of acquiring wisdom. To thoroughly understand something, you have to experience it for yourself. Don't misunderstand; the wise man can learn wisdom from other wise men. You don't have to go out and experience everything in life in order to understand that some things are good for you and some things are bad for you. Only a fool doesn't learn from others and believes that he has to experience everything for himself.

For example, only an idiot would believe that he has to truly experience an actual rattlesnake bite to truly understand that rattlesnake bites are dangerous. While it may be true that the man who has lived through an actual rattlesnake bite, has a more thorough understanding of what a rattlesnake bite feels like, that fact doesn't mean that you have to experience a snake bite to understand that you need to stay clear of rattlesnakes.

Be wise enough to acquire wisdom from those who know, without having to experience the same mistakes for yourself. While there are many truths which you cannot truly understand without experience, there are also many truths which can, and should, be understood without personal experience. Learn from the experiences and mistakes of others. Leonardo da Vinci taught, "Wisdom is the daughter of experience…Shun the teachings of those speculators whose arguments are not confirmed by experience."

He did not say you should never learn wisdom from others, or that you can't acquire wisdom from others, only that you should not listen to those whose *arguments are not backed up by experience*. It is perfectly acceptable to learn wisdom from others as long as that wisdom is based on proven experience. There are some things which you need to experience in order to thoroughly understand, and other things which you can understand by having the wisdom to listen and learn from those who truly know and who have experienced certain things for themselves.

The key here is listening to those who *truly know*. There is a Swedish proverb which states, "Where wisdom doesn't go in, it doesn't come out." You can't get water from a dry well. You can acquire wisdom from another person if that person truly has wisdom to share with you, but only if he actually has wisdom to share. Just as Leonardo da Vinci taught, he has to have wisdom backed up by experience, or the experience of others which he has learned from over the years.

Even then, it is not truly *your wisdom* until you internalize what you have learned from someone else, or from your own experiences, and make it *your* wisdom. This requires that you understand what you have learned from your studies and experiences. Montaigne, the 16th century French writer, wrote, "We can be knowledgeable with other men's knowledge, but we cannot be wise with other men's wisdom." You only become wise by developing your own wisdom from what you learn and what you experience.

Kahlil Gibran, author of *The Prophet*, wrote, "Learn the words of wisdom uttered by the wise and apply them in your own life. Live them – but do not make a show of reciting them, for he who repeats what he does not understand is no better than an ass that is loaded with books." Once again, you can see that you cannot truly be wise until you understand what you have learned and can apply it in your life.

Wisdom is available for everyone, but like everything else in this world, you have to work for it. The 13th century Sufi mystic, Rumi, wrote, "Moonlight floods the whole sky from horizon to horizon; how much it can fill your room depends on its windows." Wisdom is everywhere, but it is up to you how much you acquire. You have to be open to learning, understanding, and applying wisdom in your life.

You have to apply your mind, and work to obtain wisdom. Sai Baba taught, "You must dive deep into the sea to get the pearls. What good does it do to dabble among the waves near the shore and assert that the sea has no pearls?" Just like fine pearls obtained from the depths of the ocean, pearls of wisdom require you to put in the effort to find them and to use them in your life.

Confucius taught that there are three methods of obtaining wisdom, "By three methods we may learn wisdom: first, by reflection, which is noblest; second, by imitation, which is the easiest; and third, by experience, which is the bitterest." Actually, as you go through life, you will acquire wisdom by all three of these methods, if you are wise. If you aren't wise, you will have to rely only on your personal experiences for whatever wisdom you may acquire, and this is a long, hard road.

The important thing is that you make the effort to acquire wisdom and apply that wisdom in your life. As Epicurus stated, "We must not pretend to study philosophy, but really study it; for it is not seeming healthy that we need, but true health." Once again, it is important not to merely talk the talk, but to walk the walk. Don't go out and memorize a bunch of quotes and then pretend to be a wise man. Like I said before, it does you no good to have a mind full of facts or quotes that you can recite at will. All the wise sayings in the world are useless to you if you don't put them to work. You have to apply them to your daily life.

This is where self-reflection and meditation come into play. You have to reflect on your life and evaluate the different areas of your life to see what changes need to be made. Then apply the wisdom that you have learned in ways that improve your life and bring you closer to the perfection of your character, which, if you will recall, is the main objective of the warrior lifestyle. Self-reflection and meditation are how you incorporate wisdom into your life.

Baltasar Gracian wrote, "Self-reflection is the school of wisdom." You have to reflect on how you can put wisdom to work in your life. It does not happen automatically; you have to make the effort. Syrus went as far as to say, "Wisdom is acquired by meditation." It is during meditation and self-reflection that you quiet your mind and understand how to apply wisdom in your life. This brings us back to the point that wisdom is not in words, but rather in understanding and internalizing those words of wisdom.

All of the wise words and quotes in the world will not help you if you don't truly understand what the sages were trying to teach you through their teachings. As *The Hitopadesa*, a book of Sanskrit wisdom, says, "Many can speak words of wisdom; few can practice it themselves." It is pretty useless to talk about wisdom without practicing it for yourself. The true warrior has to make wisdom a part of his life. Without wisdom, the warrior cannot make the right decisions that lead him to a successful life.

It takes wisdom to see the value in living the warrior lifestyle and the value in making all of the traits of the warrior lifestyle an integral part of your life. Baltasar Gracian explained that, "With men of understanding, wisdom counts for everything." The reason for this is that it takes wisdom to live as you should. Without wisdom, people do not see the importance of living a life of excellence. To the foolish man, living the warrior lifestyle appears to be a lot of work for nothing. Only the wise man can see the benefit in living the life of the true warrior.

Even after one sees the benefit in living the warrior lifestyle, it still takes wisdom to do so successfully. Once you have the desire to live a life of excellence, you still need the wisdom to guide you to the fulfillment of that desire. Takuan Soho wrote, "Desires are brought to life depending upon one's wisdom. Wisdom gives direction to desires."

Living the warrior lifestyle takes discipline and determination. It takes work and effort. It is not about pretense or simply talking about all the benefits or character traits; it's about action. Seneca stated, "Wisdom does not show itself so much in precept as in life – in a firmness of mind and mastery of appetite. It teaches us to do as well as talk; and to make our actions and words all of a color." This is ultimately what wisdom does for the warrior. It guides him through life and shows him how to live.

But before you can count on wisdom guiding you correctly, you must spend the time to acquire wisdom. Spend time studying the wisdom of the elders and meditate on the meanings behind their teachings. It will be time well spent.

Meditations on Wisdom

Desires are brought to life depending upon one's wisdom.
Wisdom gives direction to desires.
Takuan Soho

The plainest sign of wisdom is continual cheerfulness;
her state is like that of things in the regions above the moon,
always clear and serene.
Montaigne

Boasting begins where wisdom stops.
Japanese Proverb

Learn the words of wisdom uttered by the wise
and apply them in your own life. Live them –
but do not make a show of reciting them,
for he who repeats what he does not understand
is no better than an ass that is loaded with books.
Kahlil Gibran

A man may learn wisdom even from a foe.
Aristophanes

The height of human wisdom is to bring our tempers down
to our circumstances – and to make a calm within,
under the weight of the greatest storm without.
Daniel Defoe

True knowledge does not grow old,
so have declared the sages of all times.
The Pali Canon

Great doubts deep wisdom.
Small doubts little wisdom.
Chinese Proverb

You must dive deep into the sea to get the pearls.
What good does it do to dabble among the waves near
the shore and assert that the sea has no pearls?
Sai Baba

We learn wisdom from failure
much more than from success.
Samuel Smiles

All of the far-reaching, unfaded teachings of the
ancient sages come from the same source:
the subtle truth of great oneness.
Different expressions are merely the
result of different times and places.
Lao Tzu

Besides the noble art of getting things done,
there is the noble art of leaving things undone.
The wisdom of life consists in the
elimination of non-essentials.
Lin Yutang

Wisdom is not in words;
it is in understanding.
Rumi

Chapter 8

Honor
The Warrior's Mark of Distinction

Honor: a keen sense of right and wrong; adherence to actions or principles considered right; distinction; dignity; personal integrity; strong moral character or strength, and adherence to ethical principles.

Honor is definitely the warrior's mark of distinction. As you can see by the above definition of honor, it overlaps many of the traits which I have already covered in *Modern Bushido*, but at the same time, it is a different trait altogether. I have already discussed personal integrity, moral character, and adherence to ethical principles, so the definitions of honor that I will focus on are the keen sense of right and wrong and the adherence to actions or principles considered right.

In the past, the warrior's honor was considered something that had to be defended, even to the death. Warriors fought duels to the death to defend what they declared to be an insult to their honor or to put it in today's terms, being disrespected. Noblemen and warriors, both in the East and in the West, considered it part of their duty to defend their honor if they felt that someone had disrespected them or challenged their honor in some way. These men took drastic measures to defend their honor.

In many cases these duels were not about honor at all, but more about someone's wounded pride. To fight to the death over some misunderstanding, small disagreement, or perceived insult is not truly defending your honor, but rather defending your pride. The vast majority of these duels of honor were more about defending the man's reputation, not his honor. Nonetheless, honor is essential to living the warrior lifestyle.

It is honor and character that set the trained warrior apart from the common street thug. Both the warrior and the thug have the capability of being dangerous. The difference is that the true warrior's honor dictates his actions, whereas the thug's actions are dictated only by his own selfish desires. Without honor, the warrior would be nothing more than another dangerous thug walking the streets, but with better training in the ways of the martial arts.

As the definition above states, honor is the warrior's sense of right and wrong, and his dedication to living by the principles which he considers right and just. These principles are his code of honor which he lives by and incorporates into his life. There is no specific "honor code" for the warrior. Each man must decide for himself what his personal code of honor entails, but the warrior's code of honor must be based on the character traits of the warrior lifestyle which are discussed in *Modern Bushido*.

Among these traits are courage, integrity, respect, and a strong sense of obligation and justice. I have already discussed the importance of living your life with integrity, and I will discuss the traits of courage, respect and justice in further detail later on in this book. So I will start my discussion of honor with the subject of the warrior's obligation, both to his code of honor and to his fellow man.

One of the main parts of a warrior's honor is his strong sense of obligation. It is the warrior's duty to recognize and fulfill his various obligations in life. The fulfillment of one's obligations seems to be forgotten by the majority of people in today's society, thus this is another trait which sets the true warrior apart from the average person. Most upstanding people remember certain obligations in life such as providing for their family, but for many, that is pretty much where their sense of obligation ends.

It is different for the warrior. Honor requires the warrior to take his sense of obligation more seriously than the average man on the street. Not only does the warrior feel a strong sense of responsibility for providing for his family, but he is also honor bound to fulfill his various other obligations in life. At this point, you may be wondering what other obligations the warrior has other than to be a good person and to provide for his family. Actually, those are the obligations that everyone in a civilized society should adhere to; the warrior's obligations go much deeper because of his own personal code of honor.

One of the definitions of the word *obligation* is: "something that must be done because of a moral duty." The word *duty* is synonymous with the word *obligation*. The true warrior, who takes his own personal code of honor seriously, has a duty to be true to his code. Part of that code of honor is to fulfill his duty to his fellow man. A quick and easy way to look at this duty to your fellow man is: whenever someone does something for you, no matter how large or how small, you have a duty to repay the favor. Repaying the favor is your obligation – it is as simple as that.

For example, if your neighbor spends the afternoon helping you hang cabinets in your garage, then you owe him. By accepting his help on your garage project, you have assumed a debt that you owe until you pay him back in a manner equal to the service he freely provided for you. If someone lets you borrow his truck to haul something, you owe him a debt and you should return his truck clean and fill the gas tank for him as a way of repaying that debt.

It is pretty straightforward. When someone does something for you, you are in his debt until you repay that debt by doing something of equal value for him. As I said, this is something that the vast majority of people today pay very little attention to in their daily lives. For most, they consider their obligation paid in full with a simple "thank you" and then they quickly forget the matter altogether.

Saying "thank you" is not fulfilling your debt, it is merely being courteous. The true warrior understands this and understands that he owes this person an obligation until he is able to fulfill it in a manner equal to, or above and beyond, what this person did for him. To the warrior, this is only right, and his sense of right and wrong is what his code of honor is all about. This is where the warrior's sense of justice comes into play.

Justice is simply the warrior's dedication to doing what is right. As I discussed in the last chapter, the warrior must have the wisdom to be able to make the distinction between right and wrong, and then, he must have the courage to act on what is right. This is the basis for the warrior's code of honor. He must be utterly dedicated to what is right. Sometimes, doing what is right will not be the same as doing what is easy or what is profitable, but the warrior's code of honor requires him to put what is right ahead of what is easy or personally profitable.

Walter Lippmann wrote, "He has honor if he holds himself to an ideal of conduct though it is inconvenient, unprofitable, or dangerous to do so." This statement is a great description of the warrior. It is for this reason that Mark Twain wrote, "Honor is a harder master than the law." There are many things, which the law of the land permits, which the warrior's personal code of honor does not permit.

The discussion about fulfilling your obligation to your neighbor would be a great example of this statement. The law does not require the warrior to repay his neighbor for lending him his truck or for helping him work in his garage; it is the warrior's code of honor that requires him to repay his debt. When you begin to reflect and meditate on your own code of honor, you will find that there are many examples which prove this statement to be true.

Ultimately, you determine whether or not you are honorable. Honor is not something which is set in stone or something which I can lay out for you in black and white terms. I can give you the cornerstones of honor and the guidance as to what traits make up honor, but it is up to you to determine your own personal code of honor. The key is that your code of honor has to be based on the character traits discussed in this book, a strong sense of justice and obligation, and you must have the courage to live up to your code of honor once you have developed it.

Nobody is going to force you to live your life by a code of honor; it is solely up to you. This is part of your duty as a true warrior. You have to base your actions on a strong sense of right and wrong. That is what honor is all about. It is not about a list of rules that you rigidly adhere to no matter what the situation or circumstances may be.

By adhering to a rigid set of rules, you are placing a higher value on those rules than you are on what is right. This is a warped sense of justice which many times leads to injustice. As the Roman playwright, Terence, wrote, "The strictest justice is sometimes the greatest injustice." This applies to a strict adherence to a specific set of rules, with no room for flexibility. This is not the way of the warrior.

The way of the warrior is the way of true justice, where what is right is the ultimate law and trumps the law of the land. There is an inscription in the Catacombs which reads, "The just man is himself his own law." The Greek dramatist, Menander, echoed this sentiment stating, "When you are just you use your character as law." This is the way of the warrior.

Many people see this as a license to do as they please, but that is a misconception. The key to those statements is the word *just*, which means morally correct, valid and reasonable. If someone is not just then he cannot count on his character or conscience to guide him as to what is right and what is wrong. Therefore, he cannot be his own guide. In order for the warrior to use his character or conscience as his guide, he must be dedicated to what is right, have developed the wisdom to discern right from wrong, and he must be totally devoted to living a life based on honor.

Robert Wood wrote, "An honorable man esteems his moral health too much to lower himself willingly by any act that may seem base. He is true to himself and values honor for its highest meaning...There can be no real success in life unless it is accompanied by this high sense of honor." It is this sense of honor which sets the true warrior apart from other men. This is what makes him a superior man, as Confucius described him.

You have to make your own mind up to live a life of honor. It is this decision which guides you on the path to warriorship. Samuel Coleridge wrote, "Our own heart, and not other men's opinion, form our true honor." Only you know for sure if your actions are truly honorable. Of course there are actions which anyone can tell are dishonorable such as robbing someone in a dark alley. I am not talking about those types of actions. I am referring to actions which only you know your true intentions.

It is your intentions behind your actions which determine whether or not your actions are honorable. Sometimes this is not easily ascertained by other people. Francesco Guicciardini demonstrated this fact very well in the following example from his book *Maxims and Reflections*. He wrote, "There is a difference between a brave man and one who faces danger out of regard for honor. Both recognize danger; but the former believes he can defend himself against it, and if he did not, he would not face it. The latter may even fear the danger more than he should, but he stands firm – not because he is unafraid but because he has decided he would rather suffer harm than shame."

In this example, an onlooker would not be able to visibly see the difference in the actions of these two men. It is only the men themselves who would truly know whether or not their actions were honorable. And it is not just the rare, dangerous conflicts which test your honor.

How you handle the smaller, more common challenges, also reveals your sense of honor, maybe even more so than the more dangerous situations. Compromising your honor in the small, daily conflicts is sometimes more tempting than in the larger, more serious conflicts. It is during these times, when it is easier to lie or to cower down, that you learn much about your sense of honor.

These situations require as much resolve and courage as the more serious ones. I'm talking about times when doing the right thing could cost you money or your job. At these times, your life may not be on the line, but your honor is nonetheless. Your job, your money, your car, and your home can all be taken away from you, but whether or not you keep your honor is completely under your control. It takes a lot of courage to choose your honor over your financial security. During these times you learn how serious you are about your honor.

As a true warrior, you not only have obligations to other people, but you also have a duty to yourself to maintain your honor, even in the face of adversity. This is where the virtue of courage enters into the equation. You have to have the courage to stand up for what you know is right. This is part of the warrior's code of honor. A strong sense of right and wrong encompasses every part of the warrior's life. This sense of justice dictates the warrior's code of honor.

It is this sense of justice which enables the warrior to make decisions concerning his obligations and which helps him make the right decisions during questions of honor. As I said before, honor is not black and white. The warrior does not live by a strict set of rules. This is not what having an honor code is all about. For example, the warrior's code of honor may include being honest, but at the same time, there are times when being completely honest is not honorable, or the right thing to do. I will discuss this later.

There are many people who will argue that you should never lie. They will tell you that all lies are an act of cowardice, but this is simply not true. Obligations of honor are not rigid rules which the warrior must strictly abide by or else lose his honor. The honorable warrior will always act according to *what is right in the situation* he finds himself in – according to his highest obligation of honor.

Socrates taught that, "The shortest and surest way to live with honor in the world is to be in reality what we would appear to be; all human virtues increase and strengthen themselves by the practice and experience of them." Don't merely appear to be honorable, but actually be honorable. Take your code of honor seriously. You will be presented with many temptations to compromise your honor. Don't allow emotions such as fear, greed, or anger to rob you of your honor. Nobody can take your honor from you, but you can lose your honor by giving in to these various temptations. You have to be completely dedicated to maintaining your honor or you will find that it has quietly slipped away, without you even realizing it.

Just remember, as with all of the traits of the warrior lifestyle, you will make mistakes at times. It does no good to beat yourself up when you fall short. If you find that you have fallen prey to some temptation and compromised your honor in some way, the best thing you can do is get right back on track and re-dedicate yourself to living a life of honor. You are never defeated unless you quit trying.

people with respect, even if they do not deserve true respect or admiration. I know this sounds like a contradiction of what I said earlier, but it's not. Think about it. Treating someone with respect is not the same as going through habitual motions without being thoughtful, and it is not the same as giving someone your true respect. It is simply *treating* people in a respectful manner – that's all.

William Lyon Phelps stated, "This is the final test of a gentleman: his respect for those who can be of no possible service to him." He is not talking about having a deep admiration of people who do not deserve admiration. What he is talking about is how you treat people who may not be deserving of true respect, people like the wino on the street corner. Most likely you don't have a lot of admiration for the wino who is drinking his life away, but that doesn't mean that you have to treat him with contempt.

There is a vast difference between treating someone with respect and having true respect for someone. This is where many people go wrong. When the majority of people do not respect someone, they treat that person with contempt or outright ignore him altogether. Since they have no respect for this person, they consider him worthless and not worth their time. In fact, they take the opposite approach of treating this person in a respectful manner, and treat him with outright disrespect, as if he is garbage.

This is not the way of the warrior. While there are obviously people who you will not have any true admiration for, it doesn't mean that you should outwardly show that fact. Remember, one of the definitions of respect is thoughtfulness. Respect is not only what you give to people that you admire, but it is also something that you have to earn by your own actions. The true warrior will treat everyone in a respectful manner regardless of whether or not he truly respects them.

How you treat others speaks to *your* character, not their character. It speaks to the kind of man that *you* are and the code that *you* live by. Being rude and inconsiderate to others, simply because you do not have true respect for them, is unacceptable. Of course there will be times when your outward disrespect is called for, but I am talking about generally as you go through life. Treat everyone in a respectful manner until you have a good reason not to do so, and that reason will concern personal issues and have specific purposes.

If someone treats you with total disrespect, is rude to you, etc., you have no further obligation to continue to treat him in a respectful manner. In fact, it is best to just keep your distance from him, if at all possible. It is not your duty to continue to allow someone to disrupt your life or rob you of your peace of mind. People who do these things are not worthy of your true respect or of your respectful treatment. In short, just ignore them as if they were a ghost, if at all possible.

Those people are the exception to the rule. What I am referring to here, are the people you encounter in your daily life. You will not have true respect for everyone you come in contact with in your life, but that doesn't absolve you from your duty to treat everyone in a respectful manner. You don't have to truly respect everyone, but you do owe everyone a measure of respect, which is simply being thoughtful and kind.

John Gay explained it this way, "We must respect the other fellow's religion, but only in the sense and to the extent that we respect his theory that his wife is beautiful and his children smart." This is not true, authentic respect for the other guy, but rather a respect in the sense that he has the right to his own beliefs and to live his life in his own way, as long as he is not hurting anyone else. It is not your duty to judge anyone else or their choices, but rather to treat them in the right way.

You treat people in a respectful way because that is who you are as a warrior. How they react or behave is their business; how you behave is your business. As Baltasar Gracian wrote, "The man of principle never forgets what he is, because of what others are." The warrior doesn't lower his standards of behavior because of the way other men act. He doesn't act in a disrespectful manner merely because he has had a bad day or is in a bad mood. He adheres to the standards that he has decided to live by regardless of the actions of others.

It is not the opinion of the common man that matters, but the opinion of men for whom you admire and truly respect. These are the men whose respect the warrior seeks. This only makes sense. Think about it. Do you care what the wino on the street corner thinks about you or what someone who you have great respect for thinks of you?

Don't seek to be respected by everyone, rather seek to be worthy of being respected by everyone. Conduct yourself in a manner that is worthy of respect and don't worry about what others think. You determine whether or not you are worthy of true respect. Earn respect by living by your principles and standards. Don't lower your standards.

Meditations on Respect

Never take a person's dignity:
it is worth everything to them, and nothing to you.
Frank Barron

Men are respectable only as they respect.
Emerson

He who wants a rose must respect the thorn.
Persian Proverb

He who does not have the courage to speak up
for his rights cannot earn the respect of others.
Rene G. Torres

Respect is what we owe; love, what we give.
Philip James Bailey

This is the final test of a gentleman: his respect
for those who can be of no possible service to him.
William Lyon Phelps

Seek not the favor of the mulititude;
it is seldom got by honest and lawful means.
But seek the testimony of few;
and number not voices, but weigh them.
Immanuel Kant

Without feelings of respect,
what is there to distinguish men from beast?
Confucius

Respect your efforts, respect yourself.
Self-respect leads to self-discipline.
When you have both firmly under your belt,
that's real power.
Clint Eastwood

Conduct yourself in a manner that is worthy of
respect and don't worry about what others think.
Bohdi Sanders

We must respect the other fellow's religion,
but only in the sense and to the extent that we respect
his theory that his wife is beautiful and his children smart.
John Gay

Think, feel, and act like a warrior. Set yourself apart
from the rest of society by your personal excellence.
Forrest E. Morgan

The man of principle never forgets what he is,
because of what others are.
Baltasar Gracian

Knowledge will give you power,
but character respect.
Bruce Lee

Chapter 10

Discipline
The Art of Self-Control

Discipline: training that corrects, molds, or perfects the mental faculties or moral character; control gained by enforcing obedience or order; orderly or prescribed conduct or pattern of behavior; self-control.

Discipline is vital to living the warrior lifestyle. None of the other virtues or traits of warriorhood will ever be developed to their full potential without discipline. It takes discipline to control your spirit, mind and body and bring them all in line with the standards by which the warrior has decided to live his life. Without discipline, there can be no warrior lifestyle. This might seem like an extreme statement, but it is true nonetheless.

So, why is discipline so important to the warrior lifestyle? The answer lies in knowing what it takes to actually live the warrior lifestyle. The traits of the warrior lifestyle do not magically appear in your life simply because you think they sound like the way to live. It takes a lot of time and constant effort to develop these traits, just as it takes a lot of time and work to develop your martial arts skills to a point where you are proficient with them. The warrior lifestyle takes work and dedication – it's not easy.

Without self-discipline, you will barely get out of the starting gate before you find yourself starting to make excuses for skipping workouts, for not spending time in meditation, or for not studying to improve yourself. As Jim Rohn wrote, "We must all suffer one of two things: the pain of discipline or the pain of regret or disappointment."

If you really want to live the warrior lifestyle, these are truly your only two choices. You will take control of your mind and body, and discipline them to meet your goals, or you will find that somewhere down the line, you will experience the pain of regret and disappointment for not following through with your goals. It's that simple.

This is a form of delayed gratification. Either you discipline yourself now for future rewards, which you will be proud of and which will mold you into the person you want to be, or you live foolishly, only doing whatever your mind and body dictate to you, and pay in the future when you find your goals have never come to fruition. It is up to you to decide what the future holds for you. Will you discipline yourself and live a life of excellence or will you allow laziness and malaise to rob you of the completion of your objectives?

Discipline is important to virtually every part of the warrior lifestyle. The *Dhammapada* states, "Whoever gives oneself to distractions and does not give oneself to meditation, forgetting true purpose and grasping at pleasure, will eventually envy the one who practices meditation." This is true for every undertaking. If you continually put off honing your skills, you will find that your skills will not develop, and not only will they not develop, but they will regress.

It doesn't matter what the skill is that you want to perfect, if you don't work at it, it will fade away. This not only goes for meditation, but for everything from your martial arts skills to golf. Whatever skills you want to perfect in your life, you have to discipline yourself to work at them, and if you don't, you will eventually find yourself envious of those who had the discipline to continue to work and perfect their skills. As William Arthur Ward said, "The price of excellence is discipline."

If the price of excellence is discipline, then you must have discipline to live a life of excellence, and living a life of excellence is what the warrior lifestyle is all about. Therefore, discipline is vital to living the warrior lifestyle. The famous poet, Percy Bysshe Shelley, wrote, "What we do upon some great occasion will probably depend on what we already are; and what we are will be the result of previous years of self-discipline."

You must discipline yourself to prepare to successfully meet future challenges. If you do not discipline yourself to practice and perfect your martial arts skills, when you actually need them to save your life or someone else's life, they will not be there for you. Don't think that you can rest on your laurels and still be prepared to defend yourself when you need to. It doesn't work that way. And you sure can't wait until you find yourself face to face with some thug, who is determined to rip you to threads, and ask for a couple of minutes to stretch and loosen up before you engage him. That is ridiculous!

Jim Rohn pointed out, "Discipline is the bridge between goals and accomplishments." Yet, so many people let discipline slide and still feel that they are prepared to meet life's challenges, that is, until they get to the river and find that the "bridge" that discipline was supposed to build between their goals and their objectives, never got built because they neglected to discipline themselves. Then it is too late and all that they have are their regrets.

You have to train yourself to do what it takes to compose your character, to control your mind and emotions, and to build your physical skills. It takes dedication and hard work, and many times your mind and your body will be screaming at you to do something besides work on your training. You have to have the discipline to overrule your mind, take control, and follow through to achieve your goals. This is what self-discipline is all about.

Elihu Root put it this way, "The worst, the hardest, the most disagreeable thing that you may have to do may be the thing that counts most, because it is the hard discipline, and it alone, that makes possible the highest efficiency." It does no good to only concentrate on the training that you enjoy or that you are good at and find easy; you have to work on the areas that need improvement. You have to push yourself to train and improve your weak points, even if you find that training disagreeable and unpleasant.

David Campbell wrote, "Discipline is remembering what you want." Whenever you find yourself tempted to be a couch potato instead of training, remind yourself what you really want. What is it that you want to achieve? What kind of person do you really want to be? Ask yourself these questions, and then ask yourself what you need to do to achieve those objectives.

You can look at your goals in the warrior lifestyle like a garden. In essence, you are cultivating all of the qualities that you want in your life by giving them continual attention. Just like a garden, you have to give your goals daily attention to see them come to fruition. If you start a garden and don't continue to tend to it, your goal of a good harvest will not be fulfilled. You have to discipline yourself to do the garden work, even when you had rather be doing other things, in order to have a beautiful, striving garden.

The parts of your garden that are growing well and weed free will require less work; the parts that have weeds growing and are not thriving, will require more of your time. This same principle can be applied to the development of your character traits and martial arts skills. You have to maintain the areas that you have developed well, and you have to work harder on the areas that seem to be problem areas for you.

By now, you should be starting to comprehend that self-discipline begins with your mind. You have to learn to control your mind in order to train your body to do what is needed to achieve your goals. If you can't control your mind, you will find that your self-discipline is weak. The great self-help author, Napoleon Hill, wrote, "Self-discipline begins with the mastery of your thoughts. If you don't control what you think, you can't control what you do. Simply, self-discipline enables you to think first and act afterward." Discipline your mind, and your body will follow. It is your mind that controls your body.

Abraham J. Heschel wrote, "Self-respect is the fruit of discipline; the sense of dignity grows with the ability to say no to oneself." The more you bring your mind under control, and force both your mind and your body to do what is needed to grow in the warrior lifestyle, the more confident you will become in your ability to continue to develop self-discipline. It is like a continuous cycle where the more you discipline yourself, the easier it becomes to discipline yourself. And, as you continue to take control of your mind, and develop more self-discipline in your life, the more your self-confidence, self-respect, and self-esteem grow.

Self-discipline is just like everything else. The more you practice it and the more you work at it, the easier it becomes, and eventually it becomes almost automatic. This is the point that you want to get to in your training. Make self-discipline a habit in your life. Do not let your mind, emotions, or body dictate to you how you will live your life. You decide what kind of person you want to be, and then you tell your mind and body what they *will do* and force them to do what is needed to become the person that you want to become.

It is your dedication to becoming a superior man that will motivate you to develop this kind of self-discipline. Nobody can do this for you; it is totally in your hands. If you consistently discipline yourself, you will reap great rewards. I will end this chapter with a quote by Grenville Kleiser, "By constant self-discipline and self-control you can develop greatness of character." Start to cultivate self-discipline in your life today and take control of your world. The rewards are well worth it!

Meditations on Discipline

What lies in our power to do, it lies in our power not to do.
Aristotle

What we do upon some great occasion will
probably depend on what we already are;
and what we are will be the result of
previous years of self-discipline.
Percy Bysshe Shelley

He who conquers others is strong;
he who conquers himself is mighty.
Lao Tzu

No man is free who is not master of himself.
Epictetus

By constant self-discipline and self-control
you can develop greatness of character.
Grenville Kleiser

Self-respect is the fruit of discipline;
the sense of dignity grows with
the ability to say no to oneself.
Abraham J. Heschel

Discipline is the bridge between goals and accomplishments.
Jim Rohn

A stern discipline pervades all nature,
which is a little cruel that it may be very kind.
Herbert Spencer

The price of excellence is discipline.
William Arthur Ward

The worst, the hardest, the most disagreeable thing
that you may have to do may be the thing that counts most,
because it is the hard discipline, and it alone,
that makes possible the highest efficiency.
Elihu Root

Discipline is remembering what you want.
David Campbell

Self-Discipline is an act of cultivation.
It requires you to connect today's actions
to tomorrow's results.
Gary Ryan

We must all suffer one of two things:
the pain of discipline or the pain of regret or disappointment.
Jim Rohn

Self-discipline begins with the mastery of your thoughts.
If you don't control what you think, you can't control
what you do. Simply, self-discipline enables you
to think first and act afterward.
Napoleon Hill

consequences of their words; all that concerns them is that they have been blatantly honest, and in their mind, that is all that matters.

This is a selfish, inconsiderate attitude to say the least. Many times, these people are using their honesty for an excuse to disrespect someone else or to covertly hurt someone's feelings. The bottom line is this is simply being rude and tactless. Arthur Dobrin stated, "There is always a way to be honest without being brutal." Being brutally honest is showing a lack of tact and a lack of thoughtfulness towards your fellowmen. Be honest, but do so in the right way. Like Emerson wrote, "There is always a best way of doing everything."

Another factor to consider on the subject of honesty is that, as I already discussed, honesty is a rare trait, especially complete honesty. Oh sure, most people are fairly honest about trivial things, but at the same time, they are not beyond lying when it is to their advantage. Therefore, the warrior has to become proficient at distinguishing between what is true and what is falsehood. It doesn't matter who the source of the statement is, you always have to question the validity of the statement before you accept it as the truth.

Hans Reichenback drove this point home when he said, "No statement should be believed because it is made by an authority." I will take Hans' point a bit further and state that if a statement is made by an authority, you had better give it a good examination before you accept it as truth. Those in authority are notorious when it comes to spinning the truth. It is their perceived job to control both people and the information which they allow people to know, not to be completely honest with the population. Keep this in mind.

Politicians and those in authority seem to take to heart what Baltasar Gracian wrote, "The truth is for the few, the false is for the populace, because popular." Gracian was not saying that only a very few people should know the truth, but rather that only a very few people bother to take the time to discover the truth. Politicians and leaders, on the other hand, firmly believe that it is only the few who deserve to know the truth or who can handle the truth. There is a big difference.

Gracian goes on to say, "Look beneath. For ordinary things are far other than they seem...The false is forever the lead in everything, continually dragging along the fools: the truth bring up the rear, is late, and limps along in time." The warrior has to read between the lines. He has to be intelligent enough to distinguish between the reality of things and the spin that is fed to people by the media or our leaders.

The last point that I want to make on the subject of honesty, is that, like all of the other ideals in the warrior's code of honor, honesty should always be moderated by what is right. As with all of the warrior's actions, what is right should dictate his actions, not a rigid set of rules. This brings me to the question, "Is it always wrong to lie?" Absolutely not!

There are many preachers and legalistic people who will state that it is indeed always wrong to lie. They will tell you that lying is always an act of cowardice. But they are wrong. The true warrior lives his life by his code of honor, and like I discussed in the chapter on honor, honor is based on the warrior's obligations. It is not based on any black and white, rigid set of rules, like so many people wrongly assume.

There are times when the warrior has a higher duty than to be honest with someone. For example, let's say that you were living in Nazi Germany and that you were valiantly hiding a young Jewish girl. If a group of Nazi soldiers came to your door and asked you if you were hiding any Jews, do you think that you would have a higher duty to be honest with the soldiers or a higher duty to protect the young girl? Would lying to the soldiers mean that you are being dishonest? Yes, of course you are being dishonest. Would it mean that you are being dishonorable? No!

I have heard preachers argue this point and say, "Yes, that would be dishonorable because lying is dishonest and a sin. You should just tell the truth and trust that God will protect the girl, you and your family." That argument is ridiculous. Living your life by rigid, inflexible rules is not a sign of honor; it is a sign of a lack of understanding concerning what honor truly is.

The intelligent man understands that there will be exceptions to almost everything, based on what the situation calls for and what is right in each circumstance. He strives to be honest at all times, but at the same time, he understands that doing what is right and honorable comes first and foremost in every situation of his life. Use righteousness as your guide in every decision and you will not go wrong. Righteousness trumps adherence to any one trait, rule, or law.

Always consider your highest duty and take steps to make sure that duty is fulfilled to the best of your ability. This is not being dishonest; it is being righteous. I will end this chapter with a profound thought from the ancient Greek philosopher, Isocrates, "Throughout your life choose truth and your words will be more believable that other people's oaths."

Meditations on Honesty

No statement should be believed
because it is made by an authority.
Hans Reichenbach

The truth simply is that's all. It doesn't need reasons:
it doesn't have to be right: it's just the truth. Period.
Carl Frederick

Be honest to those who are honest, and be also honest
to those who are not honest. Thus honesty is attained.
Lao Tzu

There is always a way to be honest without being brutal.
Arthur Dobrin

The fact that an opinion has been widely held is no evidence
that it is not utterly absurd; indeed in view of the silliness of
the majority of mankind, a widespread belief is more often
likely to be foolish than sensible.
Bertrand Russell

If you add to the truth, you subtract from it.
The Talmud

Instead of thinking how things may be, see them as they are.
Samuel Johnson.

Throughout your life choose truth and your words
will be more believable than other people's oaths.
Isocrates

The sky is not less blue because
the blind man does not see it.
Danish Proverb

Look beneath.
For ordinary things are far other than they seem...
The false is forever the lead in everything,
continually dragging along the fools:
the truth brings up the rear, is late,
and limps along in time.
Baltasar Gracian

Truth doesn't change because it is, or is not,
believed by a majority of the people.
Giordano Bruno

I have seldom known anyone who deserted truth in trifles
that could be trusted in matters of importance.
William Paley

Should one say that something does not exist,
merely because we have never seen or heard of it?
Ge Hung

There is no advantage in deceiving yourself.
Bodhidharma

Chapter 12

Courage
The Spirit of Valor

Courage: quality of being brave; the ability to face danger, difficulty, uncertainty, or pain without being overcome by fear or being deflected from a chosen course of action.

G. K. Chesterton stated that, "Courage is almost a contradiction in terms. It means a strong desire to live taking the form of readiness to die." Courage is one of those traits that many people seem to misunderstand. People also have a hard time distinguishing between courage and cowardice, the opposite of courage. At first, it sounds ridiculous that anyone would not be able to tell the difference between courage and cowardice, but you will understand this statement by the end of this chapter.

To begin with let's discuss what courage is. Many men have defined courage in different ways throughout the ages, and we will look at several of those definitions in this chapter. But first, let's examine the standard Webster's definition, courage is the quality of being brave and having the ability to face danger or difficult situations without being overcome by fear.

The first part of this definition is pretty straightforward – courage is the quality of being brave. But, as you will see there is much more to courage than simply being brave. The majority of people think that being brave means that one doesn't have any fear. This is not necessarily so. The man with no fear at all, in any situation, is not necessarily brave, but rather a bit unbalanced. Fear is a natural emotion, and brave men, as well as everyone else, feel the emotion of fear.

If you will notice, the definition of courage doesn't state that courage is being brave without fear. It states that courage is the quality of being brave without being *overcome by fear*. There is a big difference between having no fear and not being overcome by fear.

Having no fear indicates a total absence of the emotion of fear, which is a scary prospect in itself. If someone has a total absence of fear, his judgment will be faulty in many situations. A total absence of fear is not a virtue, but rather a mental deficiency. Fear is a necessary emotion, designed to warn us and protect us. It is only when fear becomes obsessive, and we allow fear to control us, that fear becomes a problem.

Mark Twain wrote that, "Courage is resistance to fear, mastery of fear – not absence of fear." If a man has absolutely no capability to feel fear, then he really has no capacity for courage. Courage is overcoming your fears to do what is right in the face of some danger, uncertainty, pain, or embarrassment. A man who has no fear or anxiety where danger, uncertainty, or pain is concerned, has some other mental issues going on which make him seem brave, when in actuality, what his actions are revealing are simply his mental deficiencies.

To call a man who is incapable of feeling fear brave could be compared to giving a two year old boy a hand grenade to play with as a toy. Of course the young boy would have no fear of the hand grenade because he doesn't have the intelligence to understand what it is or that it could hurt him. He doesn't have the knowledge or wisdom to understand what the dangers of this "toy" truly are, so he has no fear of it. It would be wrong to classify this boy as courageous or brave for playing with the hand grenade, when in fact, he is not displaying courage, but merely his ignorance.

The same principle applies to the man who is incapable of feeling fear. If a man does not have the wisdom to know what should be feared and what shouldn't be feared, his actions cannot be classified as courageous. He is not acting out of courage, but out of his ignorance or lack of understanding. Thucydides, the Greek historian who documented the courageous story of the Peloponnesian War, wrote, "The bravest are surely those who have the clearest vision of what is before them, glory and danger alike, and, notwithstanding, go out to face it."

If a man does not understand what he is facing, he cannot be brave in that situation, only ignorant. The difference in a courageous man and a foolhardy man is that the courageous man understands what he is up against. He understands the possible consequences of standing up for his principles, or of engaging in some physical battle, but he still acts according to his principles despite his knowledge that his actions could cost him. The foolhardy man simply acts. He is rash and compulsive, and either doesn't take the time to reflect on what the dangers are, or doesn't have the intelligence to understand the dangers.

Cervantes wrote that, "The man of true valor lies between the extremes of cowardice and rashness." Cowardice and rashness are indeed the two extremes of courage. Cowardice is a lack of courage. It is allowing fear to overcome you and cause you to falter at the time of action. Rashness, on the other hand, is being reckless, impulsive, and moving forward without giving any thought to the situation.

The one thing that both cowardice and rashness have in common is that when someone acts from either of these extremes, he is letting his emotions control his actions, not rational thought, and definitely not courage. To be courageous, a man has to be thoughtful. Francesco Guicciardini wrote, "Only the wise are brave. Others are either temerarious or foolhardy. Thus, we can say that every brave man is wise, but not that every wise man is brave."

From this point of view, we can compare courage to honor in that, it is not that easy for an outsider to judge whether or not a man is being courageous, just as it is not obvious whether or not a man is acting out of a sense of honor. If you will recall, some actions may seem dishonorable from an outside point of view, which, if we were privy to the man's thoughts and intentions, would prove to be very honorable. The same principle can apply to courage.

There are some actions which, when initially seen, may seem like acts of cowardice, but when examined closer, were truly courageous acts. At the same time, there are some actions which seem like very courageous acts, but if we were able to see beyond the obvious, we would understand that the action was not truly an act of courage at all. Let's look at a couple of examples.

First, let's look at the man with his buddies, who are about to enter into some type of physical encounter, whether it is a brawl or maybe on the battlefield. The fact that this man follows through and fights alongside his buddies, is not necessarily a sign that he is courageous. There have been many men who truly wanted to retreat, but didn't have the courage to do what their mind was telling them to do. Instead, peer pressure or the fear of what their friends would think of them, influenced their decision. Thus the decision was not made from a place of courage, but from a mindset of fear.

On the other hand, let's say you are watching an altercation at a nightclub. Two men are having a disagreement. One guy seems pushy and obnoxious, and obviously wants to fight. The other seems reluctant to fight, no matter how much the other guy pushes him.

Ultimately, the man who is reluctant to fight, turns and walks away, amidst jeers from the other man and many onlookers.

To those watching this scene, this man may seem like a coward, and indeed he may be, but the fact that he turned and walked away does not necessarily indicate that this man was a coward. He may have been a true warrior with the ability to take the other man's life at will, but instead chose to end this encounter peacefully instead of hurting the other guy. An action like that takes a lot of courage and self-confidence. This is a demonstration of self-control and courage, not of cowardice, but to the untrained eye, it probably would appear like the man was a coward.

Do you understand the point that I am trying to get across to you? Courage is demonstrated in many different ways. It is not always expressed by simply rushing in and fighting in every instance, and many times the man who rushes in and fights is not demonstrating courage. Walking away, being patient, waiting for the correct time and place, and enacting self-control are all courageous actions. There is a Philippine proverb which states, "To evade danger is not cowardice." John F. Kennedy stated a similar sentiment when he said, "Compromise does not mean cowardice."

Aristotle stated that, "The man, then, who faces and who fears the right things and from the right motive, in the right way and at the right time, and who feels confidence under the corresponding conditions, is brave." If we go by Aristotle's definition of bravery, you will observe that much of what constitutes courage has to do with what is going on inside of the man, and you are not privy to these factors. It is the internal struggle that decides whether or not a man is courageous, not merely his external actions.

You will find such ideas on courage repeated by wise men from throughout the world. E. B. Benson put it this way, "The essence of courage is not that your heart should not quake, but that nobody knows that it does." Herodotus echoed this sentiment stating, "He is the best man who, when making his plans, fears and reflects on everything that can happen to him, but in the moment of action is bold." To be courageous a man has to be thoughtful; he cannot act on mere emotion or rage. The courageous man has to be in control of himself.

Ohiyesa, when speaking of courage from a Native American point of view, stated, "The brave man, we contend, yields neither to fear nor anger, desire nor agony. He is at all times master of himself; his courage rises to the heights of chivalry." You have to think rationally and be in control of your mind to be courageous. If you aren't, your actions, while they may seem brave and courageous, are actually coming from another place, and many times this place is fear.

Courage is another of the traits of the true warrior which is intertwined with all the other virtues and character traits, for without courage a man will falter when the time comes to stand for his principles. It takes a lot of courage to do what is right when everyone around you is urging you to do the opposite. Emerson pointed out, "The test of courage comes when we are in the minority."

It doesn't take a lot of backbone to stand for your principles if you have a whole crowd of people cheering you on and patting you on the back, but it is a different story when those people are jeering at you and in your face. C. S. Lewis stated that, "Courage is not simply one of the virtues, but the form of every virtue at the testing point." The reason for this is what I just stated, when your back is against the wall, it takes courage to follow through and live up to your standards.

Confucius didn't sugar coat it when he taught, "To see what is right and not to do it is cowardice." The true warrior knows what is right according to his code of honor that he has meditated on and decided to make his guide for his life. The test of his dedication comes when he is confronted with a choice to compromise his standards or to live up to his standards and deal with whatever consequences that doing the right thing may have on his life. This is when he has to call on his courage to be strong.

Most martial artists think of courage in terms of physical confrontations. Will he have the courage to stand up and fight when the time comes and the situation requires this of him? Will he allow his fear to get the best of him and cause him to back down? These are the questions that I hear many martial artists discussing, and they are definitely valid questions. But you should also consider the question of whether or not you are dedicated enough, to your standards and your code of honor, to stand up for what you believe in when you are faced with a moral decision.

Robert Louis Stevenson wrote that, "The world has no room for cowards. We must all be ready somehow to toil, to suffer, to die. And yours is not the less noble because no drum beats before you when you go out into your daily battlefields, and no crowds shout about your coming when you return from your daily victory or defeat." Courage is not just about being brave in battle or physical confrontations. In fact, you will find many more chances to prove your courage in daily life than in the rare physical confrontation, unless you work in a warrior profession.

There is a famous quote by Shakespeare which we hear quoted very often, "Cowards die many times before their deaths, the valiant never taste of death but once." When you allow fear to overcome you, whether it is fear of pain or fear of some other consequence of standing up for what is right, you have to live with the pain of your decision for months, years, or maybe even the rest of your life. You will replay your decision over and over again in your mind, and each time you will find that the regret that you feel is a very painful experience. This is the death that Shakespeare was referring to in his famous quote.

Saint Theresa once said, "Whenever conscience commands anything, there is only one thing to fear, and that is fear." If you allow fear to control your life or your decisions, you will end up with a life full of regret. You must learn to master your fear and take control of your mind. You cultivate courage in your life just like you cultivate any of the other virtues – by working at it.

The way that you learn to conquer your fears is by confronting them. This goes back to what I discussed in the chapter on controlling your thoughts and your mind. Fear is an emotion and originates in your mind. The mind is where you must battle and conquer your fears. Each time you notice fear starting to dominate your thoughts, you have to stop and address it; if you fail to do this, your fear will gain momentum and will expand.

Face your fears and you will be able to conquer them. If you evaluate your fearful thoughts, you will notice that they all have to do with something in the future, not the immediate present. Let's go back to the example of the man walking away from a fight. The thoughts of fear that this man will have, if he is a confident man with the ability to end the fight at will, center on the questions, "What will everyone think of me if I walk away?" "Will they think I am a coward?" "Will I look weak? "Will I ever be able to hold my head up in this bar again?"

Notice that all of these questions have one thing in common – they center around what might happen in the future, not on what is happening at the present moment. Focus on what is right in the present moment, not on what may happen down the line. Of course you should consider all possible consequences and alternatives when making important decisions, but do not let fear be your deciding factor. Think rationally and always let what is right be the ultimate decision maker in your life. I will end this chapter with a thought from *The Havamal*, "The brave and generous have the best lives. They're seldom sorry." Live your life with courage and you will have few regrets.

Meditations on Courage

Be brave and courageous, for adversity
is the proving ground of virtue.
Battista Alberti

Courage is the most important of all virtues,
because without it we can't practice any
other virtue with consistency.
Maya Angelou

The world has no room for cowards.
We must all be ready somehow to toil, to suffer, to die.
And yours is not the less noble because no drum beats
before you when you go out into your daily battlefields,
and no crowds shout about your coming when you
return from your daily victory or defeat.
Robert Louis Stevenson

Cowards die many times before their deaths,
the valiant never taste of death but once.
Shakespeare

To evade danger is not cowardice.
Philippine Proverb

To see what is right and not to do it is cowardice.
Confucius

The test of courage comes when we are in the minority.
Emerson

Courage is grace under pressure.
Ernest Hemingway

The man of true valor lies between the extremes
of cowardice and rashness.
Cervantes

He is the best man who, when making his plans,
fears and reflects on everything that can happen to him,
but in the moment of action is bold.
Herodotus

Only the wise are brave.
Others are either temerarious or foolhardy.
Thus, we can say that every brave man is wise
but not that every wise man is brave.
Francesco Guicciardini

Courage is a special kind of knowledge:
the knowledge of how to fear what ought to be feared
and how not to fear what ought not to be feared.
David Ben-Gurion

Courage is resistance to fear, mastery of fear –
not absence of fear.
Mark Twain

Chapter 13

Endurance
The Warrior's Fortitude

Endurance: The ability to bear prolonged hardship, exertion, or pain; the survival or persistence of something over time.

As you can see from the definition above, there are basically two different definitions for endurance, and both are important for the warrior. The warrior must be able to withstand prolonged hardship and pain, just as everyone must at one time or another in life. In addition, it should go without saying, that the warrior must be persistent in his quest for the warrior lifestyle in order to be successful. Without a doubt, the ability to bear prolonged exertion is part of the warrior's physical training. Together these traits form the warrior's fortitude.

Henry Tuckerman stated that, "There is a strength of a quiet endurance as significant of courage as the most daring feats of prowess." Endurance does take courage. It is extremely tempting to just give up and throw in the towel when hardship and pain becomes almost overwhelming, but it is precisely at that time that the warrior's endurance is most needed. During times of persistent hardship is when the warrior learns the most about his fortitude.

You have to train yourself to endure the tough times in order to be successful, no matter what your goal may be. If you give up when the going gets tough, you will never accomplish much in life. Everyone has tough times. Everyone has periods where everything seems to go wrong and where they hear the very tempting voice of defeat whispering, "It is not worth it – just throw in the towel and walk away." The temptation to give in to defeat is felt by everybody at one time or another, but a determined fortitude and a never-say-die attitude are distinctive characteristics of the warrior. It is a vital part of the warrior lifestyle.

To put fortitude in layman's terms, it literally means, "guts, grit, determination, resilience, and staying power." Obviously, these are traits that the warrior must have, not only to be successful in the warrior lifestyle, but to successfully perfect any one of the single traits of *Modern Bushido*. Ralph Bunche stated, "To make our way, we must have firm resolve, persistence, and tenacity. We gear ourselves to work hard all the way. We can never let up." That is a perfect picture of what it takes to live the warrior lifestyle.

One of the most famous self-help authors of our times, Napoleon Hill, wrote, "The majority of men meet with failure because of their lack of persistence in creating new plans to take the place of those which fail." A vital part of the warrior's fortitude is the tenacity to not give up when he fails in one endeavor or another. Everyone makes mistakes. Everyone falls short at one time or another. The warrior lifestyle is a never-ending, ongoing process, not a goal that you achieve and then check off of your completion list.

You will fall short in one area or another as you work to perfect your character, your mental processes, and your physical skills. You will encounter sore muscles, injuries, and setbacks as you go through the process of training. The trick is to not give up. This is what it means to endure, to follow through with determination, to endure exertion and pain. If you find that your plan to achieve your objectives is not working, don't give up, simply create a new plan. To quote Napoleon Hill again, "Patience, persistence and perspiration make an unbeatable combination for success." You will find that many times a little more persistence will turn a seemingly hopeless situation into a success.

The second definition of endurance is the survival or persistence of something over time. Napoleon Hill stated that, "Persistence is to the character of man as carbon is to steel." When you add carbon to steel, you make the steel harder and stronger. Carbon makes it better. This is what persistence does with your character. Giving up weakens your character, whereas persistently enduring life's hardships builds your character.

William Barclay wrote, "Endurance is not just the ability to bear a hard thing, but to turn it into glory." For the warrior, endurance means more than simply putting up with a bad situation; it means conquering that situation and turning it into a victory. It is one thing to simply survive a prolonged hardship, but it is another thing entirely to take that hardship and turn it into something positive. That is the warrior's objective. Survival is the foundation of endurance; complete triumph is the endgame.

When speaking of survival, there are two schools of thought which go to opposite extremes. The first school of thought is when it comes to survival, anything goes. Imelda Marcos stated, "Doesn't the fight for survival also justify swindle and theft? In self-defense, anything goes." Imelda Marcos was a crook. Her statement was basically meant to justify her unethical actions. While it is true that in a real life-or-death, physical encounter, anything goes, this philosophy should not apply to enduring life's hardships. This is especially true for the warrior.

The warrior has to learn to endure life's hardships and pain, but having to endure hardships is not an excuse to lower your standards or to lose your honor. There is a right way and a wrong way to do everything. Turning to dishonest acts and justifying them by blaming them on your circumstances is merely a cop out. This is not the way of the warrior, but rather the mindset of the criminal.

On the other extreme, you have the ultra passive school of thought which basically states that it is better to die than to ever harm another person, no matter what the circumstances. Khalil Gibran stated, "If my survival caused another to perish, then death would be sweeter and more beloved." Again, this is not the way of the warrior. There are times when your survival may require that you do harm to another person. While the true warrior never *wants* to hurt or injure anyone else, he is certainly willing to do so if his hand is forced.

If his survival depends on his using martial arts skills to defend himself, then he is certainly justified. The philosophy that there is never any reason to harm or kill another human being is for monks or priests – not for warriors. Someone has to be willing to stand against evil in a proactive way, and that someone is the warrior.

The warrior lives somewhere in between these two extreme philosophies. His philosophy, concerning enduring hardships and surviving what life throws at him, has to be balanced with the code by which he lives. Surviving life's hardships does not mean lowering your standards or temporarily shelving your principles. It means using your principles to overcome the hardships you are facing and turning those hardships into a victory in the end.

Hunker down when you need to. The middle of a blizzard is not the time to take action and shovel your driveway; it is the time to patiently wait in the safety of your warm house. After the storm clears is the time to pull out the snow shovels and persistently work to clear the snow and declare victory over the storm. Going out and working to remove the snow in the middle of the blizzard is only an exercise in futility; this is not smart. Endure the storm's fury, and then take action to achieve victory and overcome what the storm has thrown at you.

Timing is important. There is a time and a place for everything. There is a time to sit patiently and a time to take action. Both of these are important aspects of endurance. Waiting patiently is not the same thing as doing nothing. Many times, patiently waiting for the right time to take action is the hardest part of enduring life's hardships. A good example of this has to do with your physical training.

Suppose that during your training, you pull a muscle in your leg while sparring. Of course you aren't going to just give up and decide to throw in the towel on your martial arts training. Persistence is a vital part of perfecting your martial arts skills, so you have to endure this painful injury and continue to train, but you have to be disciplined in doing so. You have to be patient and wait for your injury to heal before you continue your training. This is an important part of the process of endurance and persistence.

If you were to skip this phase and just continue to train, thinking that you are showing your fortitude by enduring the pain and working through it no matter what, you would simply be making things worse. Don't confuse endurance and perseverance with foolishness. Like I said before, there is a time and a place for everything, including waiting patiently for the right time to act.

Being persistent doesn't mean that you work nonstop and try to force things to happen; it means not quitting, not giving up. Neither does being persistent mean that you continue to pound away at your challenge using the exact same means. You may have to change your plans and your approach to the problem in order to ultimately be successful. Remember that often repeated definition of insanity – doing the same thing and expecting different results.

Be persistent in continuing to endure and to work at achieving your objective, not at doing the same exact thing. There is a big difference in the two. W. Edwards Deming stated that, "It is not necessary to change. Survival is not mandatory." Everything changes. Nothing remains the same for very long. You have to be willing to change in order to survive. While your core principles should not change, your actions must be flexible. You must adapt your actions to the circumstances in order to survive, and you must do so without compromising your principles. Endure the storms of life and rise above them in order to reach your ultimate goal.

Meditations on Endurance

Endurance is one of the most difficult disciplines,
but it is to the one who endures that the final victory comes.
Buddha

Endurance is nobler than strength.
John Ruskin

Sorrow and silence are strong,
and patient endurance is godlike.
Henry Wadsworth Longfellow

We too must endure and persevere in the inquiry, and then
courage will not laugh at our faintheartedness in searching
for courage; which after all may, very likely, be endurance.
Socrates

Endurance is patience concentrated.
Thomas Carlyle

There is a strength of a quiet endurance as significant
of courage as the most daring feats of prowess.
Henry Tuckerman

Heroism is endurance for one moment more.
George F. Kennan

Endurance is not just the ability to bear a hard thing,
but to turn it into glory.
William Barclay

Prolonged endurance tames the bold.
Lord Byron

The men who learn endurance,
are they who call the whole world, brother.
Charles Dickens

Come what may, all bad fortune
is to be conquered by endurance.
Virgil

Endurance and to be able to endure is the
first lesson a child should learn because
it's the one they will most need to know.
Jean-Jacques Rousseau

Endurance is the crowning quality.
James Russell Lowell

The majority of men meet with failure because of
their lack of persistence in creating new plans
to take the place of those which fail.
Napoleon Hill

Continuous, unflagging effort,
persistence and determination will win.
James Whitcomb Riley

Chapter 14

Justice
The Warrior's Conviction

Justice: the quality of being righteous; rectitude; impartiality; fairness; the quality of being right or correct; sound reason; rightfulness; validity.

Justice is the quality of being righteous, or in more straightforward terms, the quality of being right or correct. This isn't referring to being right as far as trivial knowledge, but rather being right where your actions are concerned. As I have already discussed, the true warrior does his best to ensure that his actions are right and that all of his decisions are based on what is right according to his own standards, not necessarily the legal standards of the day. This is the warrior's conviction and his dedication to integrating justice into his every action.

It is your commitment to justice that makes your actions righteous, not the outcome of your actions. You do not have complete control over the end results of your actions, and consequently, it is not the outcome which should ultimately concern you – *it is doing what is right* that is your main responsibility as a warrior. Of course you want to try your best to achieve a satisfactory outcome, but you aren't God, and you can't control everything. Your job is to be committed to justice in all your actions. Make sure that your actions are right and just, and then let the chips fall where they may.

Socrates was so committed to being just that he carried out a death sentence on his own life for trumped up charges. Even when he had the opportunity to escape, he refused because he considered breaking the law of the day unjust. This is total dedication to justice, although in my opinion, a misguided view of justice. Simply because a group of men decide to declare something a "law" doesn't automatically make their declaration just. In fact, given the character of the majority of our lawmakers, just laws are becoming a rarity.

It is for this reason that the warrior should meditate on what is truly right and wrong, and develop his own code of honor with justice as his guide. Of course that doesn't exempt him from being held accountable to the laws of the country in which he lives, but it does assure him that his actions will be just instead of simply lawful. Lao Tzu taught, "Highly evolved people have their own conscience as pure law." This train of thought is also found in the Catacombs where it is inscribed, "The just man is himself his own law."

This doesn't mean that the highly evolved, just man doesn't have to obey the laws of the land, but rather that the law of the land is not his ultimate guide or final word as far as what is just and what is unjust. The final determination comes from the warrior's internal sense of right and wrong, thus his conscience is his ultimate law. The catch here is that the warrior's conscience has to be pure, sincere, and as Lao Tzu stated, highly evolved.

Many people are not highly evolved and have very low morals. For them to depend on their conscience to guide them would be ludicrous. It is for this reason that we have to have laws at all. If everyone was highly evolved and dedicated to justice and always doing the right thing, laws would be unnecessary. But, as I am sure you are aware, this is not the case, so we elect politicians, many with no clue what true justice is, to make laws to control those who do not have the character to control themselves.

This is yet another trait which sets the true warrior apart from the average person. The general population falsely believes that justice simply means following the letter of the law. Even the wise Socrates believed this, but this is not true justice. As I stated above, the letter of the law is manmade; it is not sacred. The vast majority of our laws are enacted, not because they are dedicated to justice, but rather out of hidden agendas and backroom deals. They have little to do with justice.

Adhering strictly to some of these laws is actually injustice run amuck. It has always been this way. Aristotle taught, "The virtue of justice consists in moderation, as regulated by wisdom." Notice Aristotle said, "regulated by wisdom" not regulated by the letter of the law. The ancient Roman playwright, Terence, stated, "Extreme law is often injustice." Antoine the Healer commented, "Often man is preoccupied with human rules and forgets the inner law."

It is this *inner law* that the true warrior has to listen to in order to discern what is just and what is unjust, not rules signed into law by crooked, dishonest politicians. The warrior knows that true justice goes much deeper than these official laws. Simply because something is voted on and passed into law doesn't make it just. As Friedrich von Schiller said, "The voice of the majority is no proof of justice."

Again, I want to emphasize that I am not saying that you should not obey the law, merely that the law is not the ultimate authority concerning right and wrong to the enlightened warrior. Deliberately ignoring the law can cause you many headaches and major problems. Doing so would simply be foolish, unless you are *required* to disregard the law for reasons of higher justice or honor.

Baltasar Gracian wrote, "A just man. He stands on the side of the right with such conviction, that neither the passion of a mob, nor the violence of a despot can make him overstep the bounds of reason." This is the commitment that the warrior should have to justice, and it is also where Socrates was wrong in his decision to take his own life at the command of the Greek politicians. He overstepped the bounds of reason.

There is a big difference between being lawful and being just. Although the two can overlap, this is not always the case. Socrates was following the letter of the law, not necessarily being just. If justice was actually done in that case, Socrates would have never been sentenced to death in the first place. This is a great example of the law and true justice being at odds with each other. If you try, I am sure that you can come up with many other clear cut, modern day examples as well.

It is important for the warrior to keep this distinction in mind when considering his actions. It is also important that he keep in mind the consequences of his actions. Sometimes being just can put you at odds with the law, and that most likely will have less than desirable consequences. Although it may seem to be easy and straightforward at first glance, living the warrior lifestyle is not easy or uncomplicated. Sometimes being just requires you to make some hard decisions, but the truly just man will put what is right before what is easy.

Socrates, although I believe he made the wrong decision in the end, was an extremely wise teacher and had much to say about justice. He taught, "You are mistaken my friend, if you think that a man who is worth anything ought to spend his time weighing up the prospects of life and death. He has only one thing to consider in performing any action, that is, whether he is acting justly or unjustly, like a good man or a bad man."

Although I personally would not have made the decision to drink poison instead of escaping from prison, there can be no doubt that Socrates made his final decision based on what he thought was right.

That is the best that any man can do. Others can second guess his decisions, debate his decisions, etc., but in the end, what truly matters is that the warrior bases his decisions on what is right according to his own principles. If he does this, he has done the best that he can do and should be honored for having the integrity to do what he thought was right.

Being just is not a matter for debate. Every decision has to be either right or wrong, just or unjust. Zeno the Stoic stated, "Just as a stick must be either straight or crooked, so a man must be either just or unjust. Nor again are there degrees between just and unjust." A door is either open or shut; it has to be one or the other. It can be almost shut, but almost shut is still open. The same principle applies to your actions. They are either just or unjust. If a certain action is close to being just, but not quite there, it is still unjust.

There are many reasons that people choose not to do what is right, which in effect is choosing to be unjust. For most people, acting unjustly is merely a matter of selfishness; they are purely concerned with what is best for them personally, not in being just. This shouldn't be the case for the warrior. The warrior has to hold himself to a higher standard. His every decision is based on his perception of right and wrong. This is part of living the warrior lifestyle.

Living the warrior lifestyle requires much more than living like the average citizen. The warrior is focused on justice in all his actions, as well as his inaction. Yes, you can be unjust by doing nothing. Marcus Aurelius pointed this out clearly, stating, "You can also commit injustice by doing nothing." Gichin Funakoshi echoed this thought when he said that, "To avoid action when justice is at stake demonstrates a lack of courage."

The true warrior is accountable for both his actions and his inactions. Acting according to what is just, also includes doing nothing. "Doing nothing" is actually an action, and can be as unjust as doing something that is blatantly wrong. Pontius Pilate actually did nothing during the trial of Jesus, but his actions of "washing his hands of the whole matter" was an unjust act.

Justice is basically doing what is right without allowing your personal biases or personal desires to cause you to veer off course. This takes discipline and practice, and many times it can be a hard thing to master, but the true warrior will make it one of his priorities. As with all of the traits of the warrior lifestyle, it is important to truly make dedication to justice an integral part of your life. As Aeschylus said, "Don't appear just; be just."

Meditations on Justice

You are mistaken my friend, if you think that a man
who is worth anything ought to spend his time
weighing up the prospects of life and death.
He has only one thing to consider in performing any action,
that is, whether he is acting justly or unjustly,
like a good man or a bad man.
Socrates

The voice of the majority is no proof of justice.
Friedrich von Schiller

There is a point at which even justice does injury.
Sophocles

A just man. He stands on the side of the right
with such conviction, that neither the passion
of a mob, nor the violence of a despot can
make him overstep the bounds of reason.
Baltasar Gracian

He that is unjust in the least is unjust also in much.
The Gospel of Luke

To avoid action when justice is at stake
demonstrates a lack of courage.
Gichin Funakoshi

Often man is preoccupied with human rules
and forgets the inner law.
Antoine the Healer

Just as a stick must be either straight or crooked,
so a man must be either just or unjust.
Nor again are there degrees between just and unjust.
Zeno the Stoic

You can also commit injustice by doing nothing.
Marcus Aurelius

The just man is himself his own law.
Catacombs Inscription

The superior man enacts equity;
justice is the foundation of his deeds.
Confucius

Don't appear just; be just.
Aeschylus

Extreme law is often injustice.
Terence

The just man is not one who does hurt to none,
but one who having the power to hurt represses the will.
Pythagoras

Chapter 15

Sincerity
The Genuine Article

Sincerity: the quality or state of being sincere, honesty of mind; freedom from hypocrisy.

I have said many times that you should be a man of honor, not merely appear to be a man of honor. This means you must be sincere. You must be free from hypocrisy and develop honesty of mind, which means that you have to monitor your thoughts as I discussed earlier. No one respects a hypocrite. A hypocrite is someone who pretends to have admirable principles or beliefs, but doesn't back them up with his actions. He is a fraud. This is not the way of the warrior, but rather the way of the charlatan.

The Chinese book, *The Doctrine of the Mean*, states that, "Sincerity is the Way of Heaven…He who is sincere is one who hits upon what is right without effort…He is naturally and easily in harmony with the Way. Such a man is a sage. He who tries to be sincere is one who chooses the good and holds fast to it." Sincerity is a very important part of the warrior lifestyle and it is vital when it comes to being comfortable in your own skin.

Be who you are. This doesn't mean that you don't take pains to improve yourself and make yourself a better person, rather it means that you should be relaxed and comfortable letting people know who you truly are and what you stand for – be sincerely you. Don't worry what everyone thinks about you or if they approve or disapprove of who you are; just be yourself, and be a man of honor. Let them see what a true man of honor is like.

The key here is being a true man of honor, not simply appearing to be a man of honor. Be honorable to your very core. When you truly are the person you want to be, you do not have to be shy about being yourself. It is only when you are pretending to be someone other than who you really are, that you become unsure about allowing others to find out who you truly are.

For many people, depending on your personality, this can be a difficult thing to do. Most people desire the approval of their friends and family, and they can worry that if they allow others to see who they truly are, that they will not approve of what they see. This is one of the main reasons that people hide who they are and more or less play the part of an actor in public or around their friends and family. This usually boils down to one of two things.

First, either the person is lacking in overall self-confidence concerning who he is or how he lives his life, and fears that his peers, friends, and family will not be accepting of who he truly is or how he lives. The second factor is that he wants so much to be liked or admired, that he is hesitant to take the risk that showing his real face will cost him the respect and admiration of his friends and family.

Both of these come down to a lack of self-confidence in who he truly is as a person. While he may feel, deep down in his spirit, that he is living as he should, he has a deep-seated fear that others will not understand or approve of who he is or how he lives his life. It takes courage to live life your way, without worrying about what other people think of your choices. It also takes sincerity and making up your mind that, in the end, you are going to live your life in your own way, no matter what anyone else may think about your choices.

Anne Morrow Lindbergh points out, "The most exhausting thing in life, I have discovered, is being insincere." It is exhausting to put on an act, always being someone else when you are around other people, like an actor on a stage. It is draining because you are trying to be someone you are not. On the other hand, being sincere and being yourself means being in a relaxed, confident state of mind. Thus it does not drain your energy and you feel more comfortable.

The bottom line, where this is concerned, is that your life is *your* life. It really is nobody else's business how you choose to live your life, as long as you are not harming anyone else. If you are doing your best to live a life of honor and integrity, you have nothing to be ashamed of. Even though most people may not understand the way of the warrior, it doesn't mean you have to keep your beliefs and principles hidden or be shy about sharing your philosophy.

Living the warrior lifestyle is not something that everyone will understand, but it is also nothing to be ashamed of or to keep hidden, unless of course, you are merely pretending to live the way of the warrior and don't want anyone to know that you are a pretender. If this is the case, you have bigger issues than what others think of you, and you need to address those underlying issues and quit being a hypocrite.

you really are and living by your beliefs. If you aren't clear on what you want out of life or what you truly believe, then how can you possibly live the life you want to live? How can you be true to yourself and your principles? You can't!

Shakespeare wrote, "This above all; to thine own self be true." You have to understand yourself thoroughly in order to be true to your own self – to the beliefs and principles that you hold dear. The warrior's introspection is vitally important to his growth. The *Hagakure*, the famous Samurai book of wisdom, tells us, "Only those who continually re-examine themselves and correct their faults will grow." The key word in this quote is "continually."

Self-knowledge is not a process where you can go into meditation for a few hours, discover your true self, and then mark off it your to-do list. It, like all of the traits of the warrior lifestyle, is an ongoing process – not a one-time discovery. Self-knowledge is continuous. Nothing in this world is static; everything is constantly changing, and that includes you. Therefore, it is important that you continually monitor yourself and stay on top of the changes which take place in your life. Dag Hammarskjold stated that, "The longest journey is the journey inward." This is because that journey is not only adventurous, but also never-ending.

You will not be the exact same person this time next year as you are now. Once you develop your core principles and overall code of honor, they will stay the same for the most part, but even then, you will need to continually scrutinize yourself, your attitude, and your adherence to the life that you have chosen to live. It is up to you to ensure that you live a life of excellence and work to maintain your strengths and to improve your weaknesses. Nobody else really cares or will do it for you.

Whether or not you live a life of excellence rests solely on your own shoulders, and you absolutely cannot live a life of excellence without knowing yourself intimately. There is an old Indian proverb which states, "He who has studied himself is his own master." You must be your own master and guide your life in the desired direction.

Self-knowledge is the foundation for any improvements in your life - mental, spiritual, or physical. You have to know where you are, what your limits may be, what your current knowledge base is, and where you want to be. No matter what area of your life you focus on, self-knowledge has to be the starting point for self-improvement. Yes, this even includes your martial arts.

Think about it, you had certainly better know your initial limits before you start training, or you will end up pushing yourself too far and end up with an injury that will set your goals back. In your physical training, just as with all other areas of your life, you have to know what kind of shape you are in to start with. You have to know what your weak points are and what your strengths are. If you are very inflexible and either do not know this, or ignore this fact, and you try to throw a high kick, chances are you are going to end up pulling a muscle or worse.

Self-knowledge also plays a part in your self-defense. You must know your own capabilities and evaluate them honestly. There is a famous quote by Sun Tzu which illustrates this point. Sun Tzu wrote, "Know the enemy and know yourself; in a hundred battles you will never be in peril. When you are ignorant of the enemy but know yourself, your chances of winning or losing are equal. If ignorant both of your enemy and of yourself, you are certain in every battle to be in peril."

If you don't truly know what your abilities are and you overestimate your skills, you are putting yourself in danger if you ever find yourself in a true life-or-death situation. There is an Italian proverb which states, "He who is an ass and takes himself to be a stag, finds his mistake when he comes to leap the ditch." In the middle of a self-defense situation is not a good time to find out that you don't have the skills that you thought you had.

You have to evaluate yourself honestly when you are being introspective. It does you no good to be dishonest with yourself and fool yourself into thinking that you are something more than you actually are. Appraise yourself honestly. Only then can you see things clearly and start to improve your life. Sometimes this can be difficult to do, especially for the warrior whose skills are not where they once were.

Charles Spurgeon wrote, "It is foolish to try to live on past experience. It is a very dangerous, if not fatal habit, to judge ourselves to be safe because of something that we felt or did twenty years ago." Things change and you must be aware of those changes in your life. Perfecting your character is an ongoing process. Staying in shape is an ongoing process. Monitoring these things, understanding who you are and what you believe, and keeping track of where you stand is simply part of the process of living life to the fullest. This is true self-knowledge, and is a part of being truly prepared to live a successful life.

Meditations on Self-Knowledge

If a man does not keep pace with his companions,
perhaps it is because he hears a different drummer.
Let him step to the music which he hears,
however measured or far away.
Thoreau

We must find out what we really are
and what we really want.
Nelson Boswell

Knowing others is wisdom,
knowing yourself is Enlightenment.
Lao Tzu

This above all: to thine own self be true.
William Shakespeare

We should know what our convictions are, and
stand for them... Therefore it is wise to be as
clear as possible about one's subjective principles.
Carl Jung

It is a first principle that in order to improve yourself,
you must first know yourself.
Baltasar Gracian

One of the most important precepts
of wisdom is to know oneself.
Socrates

Ninety percent of the world's woe comes
from people not knowing themselves...
Most of us go almost all the way through
life as complete strangers to ourselves.
Sydney J. Harris

The unexamined life is not worth living.
Socrates

One may conquer in battle a thousand times a thousand men,
yet he is the best of conquerors who conquers himself.
The Dhammapada

Only those who continually re-examine themselves
and correct their faults will grow.
The Hagakure

The longest journey is the journey inward.
Dag Hammarskjold

He who has studied himself is his own master.
Indian Proverb

No man can be master of himself,
who does not first understand himself.
Baltasar Gracian

Chapter 17

Preparedness
The Spirit of Readiness

Preparedness: The state of full readiness; readiness for action; attentiveness, watchfulness, awareness, or vigilance.

Readiness for action definitely applies to the true warrior. The warrior must continually be in a state of full readiness for action, which means that he must be as prepared as possible for whatever may come his way. He must be vigilant where his preparedness is concerned, carefully examining himself daily so that he truly understands how prepared he is to meet different challenges.

Problems and challenges never come when you would like them to; they come when they come. Therefore, the warrior has to stay in a state of readiness to meet whatever may come his way. You hear many martial artists talk about how important this attitude is, at the same time, few of them seem to take this seriously. Their actions do not seem to match their words. As Emerson said, "A man's action is only a picture book of his creed." The warrior's actions should match his creed or his beliefs.

If you really believe that it is important to be prepared to handle whatever challenges may come your way, then you should believe that you must train to be prepared. There is no way that you will be prepared if you don't take action to make yourself prepared. The state of full readiness doesn't just automatically happen. You have to train to develop this attitude of mind and spirit, and the preparation of physical skills. Just like all of the other traits of the warrior lifestyle, you have to work to attain the state of preparedness.

The truth is, attaining the state of total preparedness takes more work than most of the other traits of the true warrior. In fact, it would be impossible to be prepared for every single thing that could ever happen, unless maybe your name is MacGyver. What preparedness means to the warrior is being as prepared as possible to successfully encounter whatever difficulties may come his way. It doesn't mean he is totally prepared for every single possible problem. It would be impractical to walk around daily with a backpack full of supplies ranging from a snakebite kit to climbing gear.

Although it is impractical to think that anyone can be completely prepared for anything at anytime, and will always have all the tools he needs at his disposal, you can be mentally and physically prepared for a multitude of problems. You may not walk around daily carrying a snakebite kit, but you can walk around with the knowledge of how to treat a snake bite, should this unfortunate incident take place. Part of being prepared is obtaining knowledge about many different things, and being able to recall and use that knowledge when needed.

A wide, general base of knowledge, covering many possible topics, is definitely an important part of being prepared to meet life's challenges. Many opportunities are lost from lack of knowledge. Study and learn as much as you can about many different subjects; you never know when the knowledge you obtain will come in handy or will get you out of a tight spot. Having a vast and diverse foundation of knowledge is an important part of your mental preparedness, but it is not the only piece of being mentally prepared to meet life's challenges.

Besides obtaining knowledge on many different subjects, you also have to train your mind to be prepared to handle emergency situations or physical conflicts. Being able to think rationally and stay calm in an emergency situation does not come naturally; you have to train your mind to handle high stress situations, just like you train any other part of your body. There are many techniques that you can use to train your mind to be prepared to handle life's unexpected challenges.

Meditation and visualization are both excellent tools to prepare your mind to remain calm and rational in stressful times. Also, many martial arts instructors are now moving more towards reality based training to train students to handle the different effects that stress and adrenaline have on the body during a physical confrontation. In addition, there are many breathing techniques which aid the warrior in consciously keeping his mind calm during times of high stress.

The point is you have to train your mind just like you train your body. I would recommend that you use all of the above training techniques in preparing your mind to successfully handle stressful situations. If you consistently integrate a combination of these four training techniques into your daily training, you will begin to see a difference in your mental preparedness very quickly. Let's look at each of these in a little more detail.

Although I will cover meditation is a separate chapter, I do want to give you a brief overview of it here for the purposes of mental preparedness. Meditation is very important to the warrior who wants to live the warrior lifestyle, and not just for the purposes of mental preparedness. There are many benefits to meditation, but I will limit my discussion here to how meditation helps prepare your mind to meet whatever challenges you may encounter.

One of the key skills in any physical encounter is to be able to maintain a calm, rational thought process, even when your adrenalin is pumping and you are under high stress. Meditation can help with this. The more you meditate, the more you will find your mind remains in a calm state, no matter what is happening outside of your mind. Consistent meditational practices definitely aid in keeping your mind calm and stable. It is just like any other skill; the more you practice it, the better you get at it and the more benefits you receive from it.

The key, when it comes to meditation, is consistency. You can't simply meditate every now and then and expect to see great results, anymore than you can expect to practice your martial arts every once and a while and perfect your techniques. The key to success in any endeavor is consistency. You have to commit yourself to whatever you are doing, and this includes meditation.

It is best to set aside a special time each day for your meditation practice. Also, you will want to have a special place that you go for meditation, somewhere where you will not be disturbed. By practicing at the same time, and in the same place each day, you will train your body and mind to go into meditation at this time and when you are in this place. Consistently practice meditation and you will begin to see some amazing results.

The next technique is fairly close to meditating. In fact, it is a form of meditation in itself. I'm talking about visualization. Every martial artist uses visualization, even if he doesn't realize that he is doing so. Visualization is simply seeing or visualizing certain things in your mind. If you are a martial artist, I can almost guarantee you that you have imagined yourself protecting someone, or fighting off some thug who was trying to attack you. This is a normal process of your imagination, and this is what I mean when I talk about visualization.

Visualization is basically the process of making a movie in your mind. You want to see yourself in many different situations, using your martial arts skills or your de-escalation skills to walk away from specific conflicts victoriously. The key to successful visualization is that you always see yourself being *victorious*. You don't want to visualize yourself screwing up or making mistakes. Visualizing yourself losing or messing up, is like practicing your martial arts skills incorrectly, over and over again.

In the practice of visualization, see yourself performing each skill perfectly. When you practice visualization, see all the details. See yourself saying exactly the right thing, at the right time. See yourself throwing perfect kicks and punches. See yourself successfully countering anything which your opponent throws at you. Are you starting to understand? Perfect practice makes perfect techniques, and that is what you want to develop through your visualization practice.

This brings me to reality based training. In your visualization practice, you want to make things as realistic as possible, while making sure you always win. Reality based training works on the same principle by preparing your mind to deal with real problems. In reality based training, instructors will play the role of the predator. They will get in your face, scream at you, curse at you, and try their best to push your buttons, just as some thug would do in the streets.

Even though you realize that this is role play, it still has the same effect as a real assault would on your mind. It gets your adrenalin pumping and puts stress on your mind. Sometimes it will make you angry. This is all a part of the process. The purpose of reality training is to allow you to experience these emotions and the feeling of trying to control your temper while some jerk is in your face, screaming obscenities at you and shoving you.

This is especially good practice for someone who has never experienced a real fight, but it is helpful for everyone. It gives you vital practice in de-escalating volatile situations and allows you to practice self-control while your adrenaline is pushing you to attack. It would serve you well to find an instructor who integrates this form of practice into his training.

The last technique I want to go over with you is autogenic breathing. Many people from cops to martial artists use this technique to remain calm in stressful situations. It is easy to learn and works like a charm once you have practiced it for a while. The purpose is to keep your mind and body calm, no matter what is happening outside of your mind.

Here is how it works. It is simply breathing, but with a catch. You breathe in through your nose, slowly for a count of four. Then hold your breath for a count of six, and slowly breathe out of your mouth for a count of four again. Do several cycles of this breathing pattern and you will find that both your mind and your body will become more relaxed. You can do this as often as you need to. There are many other breathing techniques to explore, but this one is simple and can be used quickly in most any situation.

While mental preparedness is vital, it is equally important for you to keep your body in good shape. We have all seen the comedian in the movies who has been taking martial arts classes, and who is unexpectedly accosted by some thug. When he is about to be attacked, the comedian says, "Hold on a minute while I stretch," and the thug looks at him as if he is crazy. In the real world, this is crazy!

Thugs attack you in order to overtake you in the fastest, easiest way possible. They hope you aren't prepared for their assault, and they certainly aren't going to give you some extra time to get prepared out of some sense of fair play. You have to be prepared before you run into trouble. You have to be preparing for this moment daily. This is what your physical training is all about. If you allow your laziness or melancholy attitude to get in the way of your training today, you will not be prepared for the unexpected challenge tomorrow.

Musashi put it this way, "Study strategy over the years and achieve the spirit of the warrior. Today is victory over yourself of yesterday; tomorrow is your victory over lesser men." What you do today determines how prepared you will be for tomorrow's challenge. To be prepared, you have to continue your training and keep your body in good physical condition. This includes weight training, stretching, weapons training, and your martial arts training.

Furthermore, if you go back to the definition of preparedness, you will notice that the third definition is: attentiveness, watchfulness, awareness, or vigilance. Being aware of your surroundings is an important part of being prepared to meet, or more importantly, to avoid, possible dangers. The concept of awareness goes hand in hand with being prepared to meet life's challenges. Awareness means noticing or realizing something, or being well-informed about what is going on in the world around you. It is also obtaining knowledge about something from having observed it or heard it.

You cannot be prepared in this world without some degree of awareness of what is happening in the world around you. In short, awareness is the way of conscious living. Too many people simply walk through life on auto-pilot, not paying attention to the world around them. You see them walking with their heads down, oblivious to everything else. They are lost in their own little world, completely focused on whatever is tiptoeing through their minds at the moment, with little care about anything else. This is not a state of preparedness.

In order to be truly prepared, you have to be mindful of what is going on around you, both in your immediate presence, and in your world in general. Being truly prepared to defend yourself doesn't merely mean that you know how to fight, but rather that you know how to avoid fighting. As Sun Tzu taught in *The Art of War*, "He is victorious who knows when and when not to fight." The master of self-defense is also a master of awareness.

Like mental preparedness, awareness includes much more than being aware of your immediate surroundings, although that is definitely very important. Awareness also refers to being aware of how prepared you actually are and knowing what your state of preparedness actually is. You need to be aware of how prepared you are to meet certain situations. Are you mentally prepared to defend yourself? How far are you willing to go to protect your life or the life of your loved ones? Are your physical skills at a point where you can defend yourself or are you merely under the illusion that you can defend yourself?

These are all questions which you have to know the answer to in order to be truly prepared to successfully deal with an unexpected physical conflict. You have to be aware of what you can and cannot do. Know your current limitations so that you don't find yourself in a tough spot from either overconfidence or foolish pride. Barry Long stated, "The state of awareness is the state in which you see things as they are." This is very important for the warrior.

It is so easy to see things as you want them to be instead of as they truly are, but this is dangerous for the warrior. You have to judge your spiritual, mental and physical preparedness soberly. It is vital that you evaluate yourself honestly. It does no good to convince yourself that you are prepared to defend yourself, when in reality, you don't have the skills you really need to be truly prepared. This self-deception is unhelpful at best, and downright dangerous at worst.

Preparedness is one of the cornerstones of the warrior lifestyle. That is why we train so hard in what is, for the most part, a peaceful society. You may never be called on to use your martial arts skills in a real life-or-death situation, but one thing is for sure, if you don't have those skills when you need them, you will be in trouble.

For the warrior, being prepared means that you are ready to handle a challenge before it slaps you across the face, not afterwards. Living in full readiness to meet life's challenges doesn't mean you are un-relaxed or always on edge; it means that you have been true to your training and that you are living in a state of awareness.

Meditations on Preparedness

The art of war teaches us to rely not on the likelihood of the enemy's not coming, but on our own readiness to receive him; not on the chance of his not attacking, but rather on the fact that we have made our position unassailable.
Sun Tzu

Let us not look back in anger or forward in fear, but around in awareness.
James Thurber

The key to growth is the introduction of higher dimensions of consciousness into our awareness.
Lao Tzu

By keeping your weapons in order, your enemy will be subjugated.
Nagarjuna

Do not be tricked into thinking that there are no crocodiles just because the water is still.
Malaysian Proverb

Survival favors the prepared mind.
Robert Crowley

Avoiding danger is not cowardice.
Philippine Proverb

The state of awareness is the state in which you see things as they are.
Barry Long

What is necessary to change a person
is to change his awareness of himself.
Abraham Maslow

For opportunity knocks at your door just once,
and in many cases you have to decide and to act quickly.
Francesco Guicciardini

You must be deadly serious in training.
Gichin Funakoshi

To be prepared for war is one of the
most effective means of preserving peace.
George Washington

He does not guard himself well
who is not always on his guard.
French Proverb

Tomorrow's battle is won during today's practice.
Samurai Maxim

Even in the sheath the knife must be sharp.
Finnish Proverb

Meditations on Benevolence

One kind word warms three winter months.
Japanese Proverb

Never lose a chance of saying a kind word.
William Makepeace Thackeray

We should give as we would receive,
cheerfully, quickly, and without hesitation;
for there is no grace in a benefit that sticks to the fingers.
Seneca

If you have much give of your wealth,
if you have little give of your heart.
Arab Proverb

To a person struggling in the sea of life a
few uplifting words may be of great help.
Sai Baba

I expect to pass through life but once.
If, therefore, there be any kindness I can show,
or any good thing I can do for my fellow being,
let me do it now…as I shall not pass this way again.
William Penn

Have benevolence towards all living things.
The Tattvartha Sutra

Compassion is the basis of morality.
Arnold Schopenhauer

Take the trouble to stop and think of the other person's
feelings, his viewpoints, his desires and needs. Think more
of what the other fellow wants, and how he must feel.
Maxwell Maltz

Do not let the ingratitude of many men deter you from doing
good to others. To do good without ulterior motive is
a generous and almost divine thing in itself.
Francesco Guicciardini

The little I have seen of this world teaches me to look
upon the errors of others in sorrow, not in anger.
Henry Wadsworth Longfellow

You cannot do a kindness too soon,
for you never know how soon will be too late.
Emerson

Remember there's no such thing as a small act of kindness.
Every act creates a ripple with no logical end.
Scott Adams

Meditations on Spirituality

We must walk in balance on the earth –
a foot in spirit and a foot in the physical.
Lynn Andrews

Do not become attached to this temporary physical body;
use the body as a tool. Consider yourself as separate
from this destructive body, which has been created
out of the blending of the five elements.
Sai Baba

It is perfectly certain that the soul
is immortal and imperishable,
and our souls will actually exist in another world.
Socrates

Truth is one; only It is called by different names.
Ramakrishna

God enters by a private door into every individual.
Emerson

Apprehend God in all things, for God is in all things.
Meister Eckhart

There is only one Universal Way,
but from different perspectives it is given different names.
Lao Tzu

All things share the same true nature.
Bodhidharma

When the One Great Scorer comes to write
against your name, He marks, not that you
won or lost, but how you played the game.
Grantland Rice

Know that you are always in God's Presence.
The Kabbalah

We are all children of the one God.
God is listening to me.
The sun, the darkness, the winds,
are all listening to what we now say.
Geronimo

The Great Spirit sees and hears
everything, and He never forgets.
In-Mut-Too-Yah-Lat-Lat

For the kingdom of God is within you.
Jesus

Tao is the Being that resides in all beings.
Tai Gong Diao

Man sees only what is visible,
but the Lord sees into the heart.
The Book of Proverbs

Chapter 21

Meditation
The Inner Secret

Meditation: The emptying or concentration of mind: the emptying of the mind of thoughts, or the concentration of the mind on one thing, in order to aid mental or spiritual development, contemplation, or relaxation; pondering of something: the act of thinking about something carefully, calmly, seriously, and for some time.

Meditation carries two meanings for the warrior and both are important in his quest to live the warrior lifestyle. The most common definition of meditation is that of sitting quietly and emptying the mind of outside thoughts. The other definition is contemplating or carefully considering something. This is commonly what people mean when they say that they will meditate on a question or a problem. The true warrior should integrate both forms of meditation into his life. Let's look at the second definition first.

There are many things which the warrior must give some serious thought to concerning the warrior lifestyle. From seriously thinking about what he truly believes to pondering why he holds certain principles to be important, the warrior spends more time meditating on what is important to him than the average person. The average, everyday guy mostly goes through life without giving these things much thought, doing whatever gives him pleasure or whatever he finds himself in the mood for at the moment.

As I have said before, the warrior takes the things in his life a bit more seriously than the average guy. He knows the importance of spending quality time meditating on his principles and developing his own personal codes – his code of honor and his code of ethics. This takes time spent alone with his thoughts, in quiet contemplation. He has to shut out all of the outside distractions and focus his mind seriously on the topic at hand. With all of the outside distractions which we all have at our fingertips, this is something that is easier said than done.

I must also make an important distinction concerning meditating on your problems or objectives. Giving serious thought to an issue is not the same thing as constantly worrying about it. Worrying about a problem is never constructive or helpful. Actually, worrying about a problem only causes you more stress and prevents you from being able to develop a rational strategy to improve your situation. This is not what I mean when I say that you should seriously think about a problem or solution.

If you will notice, the last definition of meditation, at the top of the previous page, is the act of thinking about something carefully, calmly, seriously, and for some time. This is vastly different from worrying about it, which is more along the lines of thinking about something in a semi-panicked state and replaying everything that *could* happen, over and over again in your mind. See the difference? Meditating on something is done in a careful, purposeful way, calmly, seriously, and rationally. Worrying doesn't include any of those characteristics.

Yes, this can be hard to do, especially when the challenge you are facing is serious and carries with it some serious consequences, but it is also important to develop this ability. Which brings me to the question of how do you learn to develop this ability? How is one able to control his thoughts and his mind? The answer is meditation. I know, this sounds a bit like a Zen koan. How do you learn to control your mind and meditate on a specific topic? You learn to successfully meditate on something by learning the art of meditation.

In this case, I am referring to the first definition of meditation – the art of emptying the mind. There are many advantages to meditation. Meditation lowers your stress level, decreases anxiety (worry), decreases depression, irritability and moodiness, improves memory and learning ability, improves creativity, aids in focusing the mind, increases emotional stability, and has many other health benefits which I won't list here.

As you can clearly see, traditional meditation can indeed help you learn to control your mind and focus more successfully on whatever issue you need to focus on to find the answers you seek. Thus, you learn to successfully meditate (contemplate) on something by learning the art of meditation. There are many books, CD's and DVD's on the market which teach you how to meditate, and there are many different meditation techniques that you may want to learn.

The easiest way to start meditating is to start slow, with very short sessions, 5-10 minutes at a time. Just sit in a comfortable position, with your spine straight, and clear your mind of all thoughts. While this may sound easy, it can be a challenge. Thoughts will continually enter your mind. Just let them go. The trick is to acknowledge them but refuse to think about them. When you notice a thought has entered your mind, refuse to dwell on it – just let it fade away. Soon you will find that this process gets easier and easier, and then you can meditate for longer periods of time.

There are also other kinds of meditations. You can successfully empty your mind by focusing on a single point such as a candle flame or a mandala. These kinds of meditations involve staring at a specific point and concentrating your focus on that one point, clearing your mind of everything but the object, and just letting your mind go blank. Another meditation to help you control your thoughts is to focus on your breathing and count your breaths as they slowly go in and out.

There are too many techniques to learn for me to cover them all in this short chapter, but I do want to mention one other one before I move on – guided meditations. There is a company called Brain Sync which produces meditation CD's which are recorded at specific frequencies to induce specific brainwaves. These CD's have both a guided track and a track with only music or sounds, and are excellent for both the novice and the more experienced practitioner.

This is merely a very quick overview of meditation techniques and what meditation is. I suggest you do some research on the art of meditation and experiment with different techniques until you find the technique that fits your style and that you are comfortable using on a regular basis. And yes, you should get in the habit of meditating on a regular basis, daily is best. Once you get the art of meditation down, I recommend meditating once in the morning and once at night.

While meditation tends to be a part of the warrior lifestyle that many warriors neglect, it shouldn't be. They wrongly look at mediation as some "new age mumbo-jumbo" and think that it is a waste of time that they could be using in their martial arts training or some other physical activity. This is wrong thinking. I listed only a few of the benefits that meditation provides for the warrior; there are many more.

Meditation helps the warrior to control his thoughts and his mind, and to remain calm during stressful situations. The more that you meditate, the more you will find that you are able to think rationally, no matter what is happening around you. As Sai Baba stated, "Without mediation, it is not possible to control and master the mind." Controlling your thoughts and your mind is vitally important to the warrior, as I discussed in the chapter on rational thought.

If your mind is in turmoil, you can't think rationally and it will be hard to make good, clear decisions. Meditation is the solution to this problem. Margolis stated, "Only in quiet waters things mirror themselves undistorted. Only in a quiet mind is adequate perception of the world." Lao Tzu echoed this philosophy teaching, "Muddy water, let stand, becomes clear."

When you have a problem to solve and need to figure something out, sit in meditation and let the waters of your mind clear. Continually trying to solve the problem by going over and over it in your mind is like trying to clarify muddy water by continuing to splash around in it; it doesn't work. To clear the muddy water, you must let it sit quietly for a while and it will clear up on its own. The same principle applies to your mind. When you have a problem that you can't figure out, you need to step away from it for a while, quiet your mind, meditate, and let the answer come to you.

I want to touch on one more mediation technique called visualization. Most martial artists don't even realize that visualization is a form of meditation, but it is. Visualization is seeing a specific image in your mind. It can be a single image of something or watching a sequence of actions, kind of like playing a movie in your mind where you are the director, and most likely the hero.

The practice of visualization is a form of mental practice for the warrior. It is a way to put yourself in different scenarios and see yourself using your martial arts skills or perfecting the art of de-escalation. To use visualization techniques you simply play the scene over and over in your mind.

The more you practice meditation, the more benefits you will see from your endeavors. You will find that your whole demeanor is calmer and you are better able to handle stressful situations. Things that used to stress you out will no longer bother you as much. You will be able to think more clearly. Your temper will become less of a problem. This list could go on and on. The point is, meditation is a vital practice for the true warrior.

Hopefully you have grasped the importance of meditation in your life and will put it to good use. As the Dhammapada states, "Whoever gives oneself to distractions and does not give oneself to mediation, forgetting true purpose and grasping at pleasure, will eventually envy the one who practices mediation."

true goals or motivations. The wise man has to read between the lines, using logic and rational thought, to figure out others' true intentions.

This may sound a bit paranoid, but it is very important. If you take everything at face value, you will find that you are being deceived over and over again. The art of discernment is crucial for the warrior. This is even truer when it comes to life-or-death situations. If you are targeted by a predator, you have to be able to discern his true intentions, how dangerous he is, what he really wants, if he is mentally stable, etc. in order to know how to respond to de-escalate the situation. Without insight into the other person, you are merely taking a chance with whatever response you take.

It is insight and being able to read a person that gives you the advantage. I call this an art because that is exactly what it is. There are many books on the market which teach how to read people's expressions, body language, speech patterns, eyes, etc. Law enforcement officers are trained to discern certain things in people that tip them off as to whether or not someone is telling the truth or lying. I highly recommend that you do a little research on this subject.

Although, as I said, this is not any kind of mystical, psychic skill, developing accurate insight into a person's mind, a specific situation, or a specific subject, is not always a rational skill. You have to learn to trust your instinct and your intuition. Your intuition can be likened to your gut feeling. If you have a bad feeling about something, always take that feeling seriously, even if there is no rational explanation for it.

Blaise Pascal wrote that, "The heart has reasons which reason cannot understand." This is very true. Your intuition comes from your spirit, which many people believe is directly connected to God. Clear perception essentially comes from two sources: your rational ability to read between the lines and your intuition. These two sources can work together or they can be completely independent of each other, but they are both important in developing clear insight.

The sages throughout the ages have always taught that we should listen to our intuition. Sometimes this is referred to as listening to your heart or listening to your spirit. It doesn't matter what label you put on it, you should always listen to the still, quiet voice inside your mind. Gracian stated, "Trust your heart…for it is never untrue to itself." Emerson echoed this sentiment saying, "Trust the instinct to the end, though you can render no reason." Antoine de Saint-Exupery agreed stating, "It is only with the heart that one can see rightly; what is essential is invisible to the eye."

Listening to your intuition and acting according to what your spirit tells you, is not a natural thing for most people. This is especially true for the warrior, who can be more comfortable figuring things out rationally than going with his feelings. It is a process that takes practice and faith. You have to learn to trust your intuition just like you learn to trust in any of your other skills. As with listening to another person, listening to your intuition requires that you actually *listen*. Your intuition is not going to force you to listen. You have to slow down, quiet your mind, and purposely listen to what your spirit is telling you.

As you have probably figured out by now, the traits of the warrior lifestyle are all connected in one way or another. Developing insight and listening to your intuition is greatly aided by meditation. To once again quote Margolis, "Only in quiet waters things mirror themselves undistorted. Only in a quiet mind is adequate perception of the world." When you can't quite figure things out in your mind, get quiet and meditate on the situation and allow your spirit to provide you with the insight that you need.

There is an Omaha Maxim which states, "Ask questions of your heart, and you will receive answers from your heart." If indeed your spirit is directly connected to God, as many religions and sages have taught throughout the ages, then your spirit contains all the information that you need for clear insight into any situation, and it is up to you to be quiet and listen for the answers you seek. The Sufi mystic, Rumi, wrote, "Moonlight floods the whole sky from horizon to horizon; how much it can fill your room depends on your windows."

The ability to develop insight depends on you. The Zen Buddhist teacher, Dogen, taught, "Don't follow the advice of others; rather, learn to listen to the voice within yourself." Notice he said that you have to *learn to listen*. This is a skill and you have to practice it in order to perfect it. Developing this skill will prove extremely valuable to the warrior in many ways. It is not simply a useful self-defense skill, but is a skill that you can use in every part of your life, once you develop it, learn to listen, and trust what you hear.

I will end this chapter with a quote by La Rochefoucauld, "Countless acts that seem ridiculous have hidden reasons that are exceedingly wise and sound." It is insight which provides you with these *hidden reasons which are wise and sound*. Develop the art of discernment and see for yourself the value of this internal skill.

a true friend or merely an acquaintance. You should always judge someone's character before you decide to embark on a friendship.

Your choice of friends says a lot about you. Gracian tells us that, "One is known by the friends he keeps." John Caspar Lavater goes into even more detail stating, "He is a good man whose intimate friends are all good, and whose enemies are decidedly bad." Choosing to associate with people of low character is a way to guarantee that you will not be developing a true friendship, at least not with those people. Someone has to have character and honor to stand by his friends in the bad times, and people of low character do not have what it takes to be trusted to do this.

It takes time to develop a true friendship and to know for sure that you can trust someone. Even after years of companionship, you have to be careful about being too trusting. Trust has to be earned and friendship has to be proven. Until you know for certain that someone is your tried and true friend, you should be careful how much trust you place in him.

Too many people are fickle and dishonest, this may sound cold and distrustful, but it is also very true. Don't be too quick to consider someone your friend. At the same time, once you have given your friendship to someone, you have given your bond to them. As *The Havamal* says, "Be your friend's true friend." For this reason, you should be careful and slow about extending your hand in true friendship. Socrates put it perfectly, "Be slow to fall into friendship, but when you are in, continue firm and constant."

Once you have given your hand in friendship, you still have to work to make the friendship strong and to keep it strong. Like all other parts of the warrior lifestyle, friendship takes effort and work. You could look at friendship like planting a garden. If you take care of it and do your part, it will grow and flourish; if you neglect it, weeds will appear and choke what you worked hard to grow. Planting the seed of friendship is merely the first step, you have to nurture what you have planted in order for it to fully mature into a *real* friendship.

Becoming friends with someone is only the first step. You have to continually strengthen the friendship or it will begin to fade away. Emerson wrote, "Go often to the house of thy friend, for weeds choke the unused path." It is also important to remember that simply because someone is your friend, that doesn't mean that you neglect your manners and treat him anyway you want. Friendships are much easier to destroy than they are to build.

If anything, you should treat your true friends better than you do your acquaintances. They are much more important people in your life than people who you barely know and merely do business with throughout your life. There is an English proverb that illustrates this point very well, "An hour will destroy what it took an age to build." This is very true. Building a friendship takes a lot of time, patience, effort, and work, but ending a friendship takes very little effort at all.

Of course, this shouldn't be the case for the true warrior. When the warrior gives his hand in friendship, it basically takes a betrayal for him to end the friendship. He is a man of honor and takes the sacred bond of friendship seriously, and it is hard for him to comprehend that other people do not have the same dedication to friendship that he has. This can lead to the warrior being blindsided if he is not very careful in his choice of friends. History is full of examples that show the treachery of false friends.

This is why Baltasar Gracian taught that you should, "Trust in today's friends as if they might be tomorrow's enemies." Many years before Gracian's time, the Vikings wrote this same admonition, "A man must be watchful and wary as well, and fearful of trusting a friend." Not everyone takes the sacred brotherhood of friendship as serious as the warrior does, so it is wise to be careful when it comes to trusting others.

The wisest path to take is to never trust someone with enough information to hurt you. At least not unless there is a very good reason to do so, you have known them for years, and they have proven to be a true friend through the storms of life. Even then it is wise to be careful concerning what you share. It is always best to keep some things private. Remember, even Jesus was betrayed by someone he thought was one of his closest friends.

Strive to make sure that your true friends are men of character, honor, and integrity. It is someone's character that truly matters when it comes to friendship. Look at what is inside someone when you are thinking of befriending him. Lieh Tzu put it wonderfully saying, "Ordinary people are friendly to those who are outwardly similar to them. The wise are friendly with those who are inwardly similar to them." Think about this.

I will end this chapter with another quote from La Rochefoucauld, "A true friend is the most precious of all possessions and the one we take least thought about acquiring." Take the sacred brotherhood of friendship seriously and strive to make friends of the highest quality.

Meditations on Filial Duty

The young rely on their fathers, the old on their children.
Vietnamese Proverb

You must not expect old heads upon young shoulders.
English Proverb

When you have your own children you will
understand your obligation to your parents.
Japanese Proverb

He who does not honor his wife dishonors himself.
Spanish Proverb

Show parents respect with love and devotion.
It is a tribute you should offer them for the great
chance they gave you to come into this world...
Sai Baba

Duty to parents is higher than
the mountains, deeper than the sea.
Japanese Proverb

Conduct yourself toward your parents as you would
have your children conduct themselves toward you.
Isocrates

He (Cato) never said anything obscene in front of his son,
no more than if he had been in the presence
of the holy Vestal Virgins.
Plutarch

You must apply yourself seriously to your work,
serve your parents with filial piety, behave with
propriety towards your wife…Furthermore,
as a parent you should conduct yourself with
dignity and in accordance with what is right.
Takuan Soho

A father…
He should make himself worthy of respect
by his virtue and abilities, and worthy of
love by his kindness and gentle manners.
Montaigne

Diogenes struck the father when the son swore.
Robert Burton

A torn jacket is soon mended;
but hard words bruise the heart of a child.
Henry Wadsworth Longfellow

He preaches well that lives well.
Cervantes

As iron is worn away by frequent filing,
a family's strength is eroded by incessant inner frictions.
Tiruvalluvar

Chapter 26

Balance
The Art of Harmony

Balance: A state of emotional and mental stability in which somebody is calm and able to make rational decisions and judgments; a state in which various parts form a satisfying and harmonious whole and nothing is out of proportion or unduly emphasized at the expense of the rest.

Balance is very important, both to the warrior and to the warrior lifestyle. It is extremely easy to get caught up in whatever endeavor your mind is currently focused on, and to let other important things slide. If this happens consistently, your life can quickly become unbalanced and out of harmony. The key to maintaining a state of emotional and mental stability is preserving balance in your life.

For the warrior, balance refers to keeping the three main parts of your life balanced and in harmony – spirit, mind and body. You can think of these three parts of your life as an equilateral triangle. Each side of this triangle represents one of these parts of your life and when your life is in balance, each line of this triangle should be the same length. When one line becomes longer because you are spending too much time on that part of your life or shorter because you are neglecting a part of your life, the triangle (your life) is no longer balanced.

It is a constant balancing act to keep these three parts of your life balanced and in harmony. As the definition above states, you have to work to ensure that nothing is out of proportion or overly emphasized at the expense of the other parts. Your life can easily get out of balance when you start something new and are very excited about your new interest.

For example, maybe you have been a martial artist for many years, but have never addressed the spiritual side of your life. You begin to read and study to develop your spiritual side, and find it extremely interesting, then you realize that you have basically put your martial arts training on a shelf and you are spending all of your time reading and meditating to develop your new found interest. Your spiritual line is getting too long and your physical line is suffering because of it and your life is beginning to become unbalanced.

There is absolutely nothing wrong with studying and developing your spiritual side, in fact, you should be doing this as it is part of the warrior lifestyle. But you shouldn't spend all of your time on this one area. Anytime you spend an excessive amount of time concentrating on one area, it will be at the expense of some other part of your life. The key is not to go overboard with anything that you are doing. The warrior lifestyle has many areas which must be addressed, and you shouldn't sacrifice one area in order to focus on another.

This is what balance is all about – organizing your life in such a way as to be able to develop every part of your life to the fullest. There are no unimportant traits of the warrior lifestyle. Hazrat Inayat Khan stated, "The secret of life is balance, and the absence of balance is life's destruction." You must learn to balance all the parts of your life, and while this sounds relatively easy, it takes quite a bit of discipline.

The *Talmud* teaches us to, "Be moderate in all things." Moderation is the key to balance. Epictetus taught, "If one oversteps the bounds of moderation, the greatest pleasures cease to please." Everything in life can be taken to extremes. There is basically no interest, hobby, or skill on this earth, which someone, somewhere doesn't take to the extreme. While it is not wrong to spend time and effort perfecting whatever you do, you must be careful not to do so at the expense of other important parts of your life.

Taking things to the extreme is the cause of many heartaches and regrets in this life. A good example of this would be the man who spends all his time focused on his work, at the expense of his family life. While he may become a gigantic success at work, his family life suffers for it and he may in fact find that he has sacrificed his marriage and his relationship with his children in order to spend so much time becoming a success at his job. In essence, his life is out of balance, and eventually his unbalanced life will cost him dearly.

Epicurus taught us to, "Be moderate in order to taste the joys of life in abundance." Moderation means that you intentionally limit yourself, you don't go to extremes. This doesn't mean that you never go all out and put your entire soul into something at times, but rather that you make sure that you balance these times in your life. W. Somerset Maugham wrote, "Excess on occasion is exhilarating. It prevents

Chapter 27

Excellence
The Spirit of Kaizen

Excellence: The quality or state of being outstanding and superior.

Living a life of excellence is essentially what the warrior lifestyle is all about. The true warrior should seek excellence in everything that he does whether it is gardening or his martial arts. As Ralph Marston wrote, "Excellence is not a skill. It is an attitude." It is an attitude, an attitude towards everything you do in life, and it is this attitude which makes the warrior a superior man.

The Japanese have a term called kaizen which means constant, never-ending improvement. This is what the warrior should shoot for in every area of his life – constant, never-ending improvement. No matter how well you have mastered any skill, there is always room for at least a little more improvement. Booker T. Washington stated, "Excellence is to do a common thing in an uncommon way." This is how the true warrior does everything in his life.

The vast majority of people in this world merely do the minimum. Their attitude seems to be that good enough is good enough. Good enough is rarely good enough for the warrior; he seeks perfection and excellence. This doesn't mean that everything that he does will be done to perfection, but he will at least try his best to do everything he does to the best of his ability. He puts his whole heart into whatever he may be working on at the time.

This is something that he requires of himself. Nobody is going to make you live a life of excellence. Nobody is going to hound you to be the best that you can be in life. This is a choice that you have to make. Aristotle even stated this saying, "Excellence, then, is a state concerned with choice." As the definition states, excellence is the state of being outstanding and superior. Throughout *Modern Bushido*, I have referred to the warrior as the superior man, and this is the reason for that.

The term "superior man" is not a snobbish term that is used to signify that the warrior considers himself above others and looks down on other people. This is not what is meant by that term at all. It simply means that the warrior is a man of excellence that does the best that he can do in every area of his life to integrate excellence into everything that he does. It is this attitude, combined with the correct action to transform this attitude into something tangible, which makes the true warrior a superior man – a man of excellence.

The famous football coach, Vince Lombardi, stated, "The quality of a person's life is in direct proportion to their commitment to excellence, regardless of their chosen field of endeavor." This definitely holds true for the warrior. It is his commitment to excellence that determines the quality of his life. Furthermore, it is his commitment to excellence that determines whether or not he is truly living the warrior lifestyle as he should be living it. The warrior lifestyle is not a lifestyle to be lived halfway.

Living the warrior lifestyle halfway is merely pretending to live this lifestyle of excellence. John W. Gardener stated that, "Excellence is doing ordinary things extraordinarily well." This is exactly what the superior man tries to do. Whatever he is doing, he tries to do it in an extraordinary way. This can apply to anything and everything that you do. Gardener went on to say, "Whoever I am, or whatever I am doing, some kind of excellence is within my reach." This is the true attitude of the superior man.

Excellence is a way of life. I use this quote by Henry Ward Beecher quite often, but it is a perfect motto for the true man of honor, "Hold yourself responsible for a higher standard than anyone else expects of you. Never excuse yourself." If you continually do this, you will soon find that your life is full of excellence in ways that you may not even realize. Others will see it and recognize you as a man of excellence, and it will become a part of your overall reputation, which is a great reputation to have.

Holding yourself to a higher standard is a great way to start being a man of excellence. Like I stated, living a life of excellence is a choice, nobody else is going to hold you to this standard; it is totally up to you. You have to be the one that holds yourself to this higher standard, and this goes for all of the traits that I have discussed in *Modern Bushido*. Nobody is going to force you to live the warrior lifestyle. Other people don't really care how you live as long as you aren't disrupting their lives in some way. They really don't care if you live like a street bum or a king. How you live your life is totally up to you.

To quote Aristotle again, "Excellence is an art won by training and habituation. We do not act rightly because we have virtue or excellence, but we rather have those because we have acted rightly. We are what we repeatedly do. Excellence, then, is not an act but a habit." I have to agree. Overall, excellence becomes a habit, just like everything else that you repeatedly do in your life. Each action merely reinforces your dedication to excellence or your lack of dedication to excellence. As Anne Byrhhe wrote, "Every action we take, everything we do, is either a victory or defeat in the struggle to become what we want to be."

When you decide to do something halfway, that decision in and of itself is akin to taking a step away from being a man of excellence. On the other hand, every time you slow down and make the effort to do something the best you can, then you are re-enforcing excellence in your life. As Aristotle said, excellence becomes a habit. Habits are formed by continually being consistent at whatever you are doing. The experts tell us that you can form a new habit in about a month, that is, if you are consistent with your actions.

All it takes is a firm decision to start doing everything you do, the best that you can do it. Thomas J. Watson wrote, "If you want to achieve excellence, you can get there today. As of this second, quit doing less-than-excellent work." This makes sense. If you quit doing "less-than-excellent work" everything you do will be done at a high level. Essentially, everything you do will be done at the level of excellence that you are shooting for.

Confucius put it this way, "The will to win, the desire to succeed, the urge to reach your full potential...are the keys that will unlock the door to personal excellence." You have to choose excellence as an act of your will. Living a life of excellence is pretty simple – you merely choose to do so, and then you do it. The catch is, you then have to discipline yourself to actually follow through.

Every year, thousands of people make New Year's resolutions, and at the same time, every year thousands of people fail to follow through with those resolutions. You can say that you are going to start living a life of excellence every single day, but it is meaningless if you don't back up that decision with your actions and actually start integrating excellence into your life. Like everything else in life, this takes discipline and effort.

The Greek poet, Hesiod, wrote, "Badness you can get easily, in quantity; the road is smooth, and it lies close by, but in front of excellence the immortal gods have put sweat, and long and steep is the way to it." Making a decision to live a life of excellence, and living a life of excellence are two different things. Just like writing down your New Year's resolution and actually following through with it, are two different things. Like Hesiod wrote, it takes a lot of work and effort to become a man of excellence.

Excellence has to become the prevailing attitude in your life. It actually does have to become a habit, and, as with everything else in life, you have to start from where you are. Start small and continue to build this attitude in your life. You don't decide to start martial arts training one day, and enter the ring with experts the next week. It takes time, it takes work and it takes consistent training. The same principle applies to anything you do in life. Nobody becomes an expert at anything overnight.

Colin Powell stated, "If you are going to achieve excellence in big things, you develop the habit in little matters. Excellence is not an exception it is a prevailing attitude." I discussed earlier that you have to take control of your thoughts. This is an important part of developing excellence in your life. Your thoughts are the beginning of your actions; therefore it is vital that you get your mind straight first. If your mind is not right, you will never be able to become a man of excellence.

Excellence is not something that you fake in order to build your reputation; it is an attitude and a way of life. Chung Yung wrote, "The superior man is watchful over himself even when alone." This is the attitude of excellence. It doesn't matter what he is doing or who is around him at the time, the man of excellence will seek to do everything to the best of his abilities. He agrees with the quote from Emerson that, "What I must do is all that concerns me, not what the people think."

Excellence is the way of the warrior. Each of the essential traits of the warrior lifestyle can be traced back to living a life of excellence. The normal, everyday, common life is void of the majority of these traits. The common man lives mainly for his own comfort and gives little attention to pushing himself to go the "extra mile" in order to live a life of excellence. Simply put, he is satisfied living an average life.

This is not the way of the warrior. The warrior is not satisfied just going through life, but rather, he wants to make his life the best it can be. Ordinary is simply not good enough. He wants to be extraordinary and takes the needed steps to develop his life in just that way. This is what makes him a superior man. Every man is basically born equal; it is his decisions that set him apart from others.

Meditations on Excellence

Excellence is an art won by training and habituation.
We do not act rightly because we have virtue or excellence,
but we rather have those because we have acted rightly.
We are what we repeatedly do.
Excellence, then, is not an act but a habit.
Aristotle

Badness you can get easily, in quantity; the road is smooth,
and it lies close by, but in front of excellence the immortal
gods have put sweat, and long and steep is the way to it.
Hesiod

Excellence encourages one about life generally;
it shows the spiritual wealth of the world.
George Eliot

Excellence is a better teacher than mediocrity.
The lessons of the ordinary are everywhere.
Truly profound and original insights are to
be found only in studying the exemplary.
Warren G. Bennis

If you are going to achieve excellence in big
things, you develop the habit in little matters.
Excellence is not an exception, it is a prevailing attitude.
Colin Powell

Whoever I am, or whatever I am doing,
some kind of excellence is within my reach.
John W. Gardner

Excellence is doing ordinary things extraordinarily well.
John W. Gardner

Excellence is not a skill. It is an attitude.
Ralph Marston

Excellence is the gradual result
of always striving to do better.
Pat Riley

Excellence is to do a common thing in an uncommon way.
Booker T. Washington

Ordinary is simply not good enough.
Be extraordinary!
Bohdi Sanders

Excellence, then, is a state concerned with choice...
Aristotle

If you want to achieve excellence, you can get there today.
As of this second, quit doing less-than-excellent work.
Thomas J. Watson

The quality of a person's life is in direct proportion
to their commitment to excellence,
regardless of their chosen field of endeavor.
Vince Lombardi

Chapter 28

Loyalty
The Warrior's Dedication

Loyalty: The feeling of devotion, duty, or attachment to somebody or something; the quality or state of being loyal.

Loyalty is a very admirable trait, and one which is very hard to find in people today. The average person today is self-centered and selfish. He tends to focus on only what he wants or what is best and easiest, for himself in the present moment. The slogan, "Sworn to Fun – Loyal to None," describes him perfectly. The true warrior looks at things quite a bit differently, especially where loyalty is concerned.

The warrior is fiercely loyal to his word, his duty, and to his friends and family. He has an unwavering sense of dedication to the important things and people in his life. Euripides stated that, "One loyal friend is worth ten thousand relatives." This is definitely true of the warrior. Once you have gained his friendship, his loyalty is a part of the package, and the friendship and loyalty of a true warrior is priceless. He will not turn his back on you or forsake you. He is loyal to the end.

Loyalty has always been an integral part of the warrior's character. The Samurai were so loyal to their Daimyo (feudal lord), that they would actually commit seppuku (ritual suicide) if their Daimyo commanded them to do so. This is total loyalty. In the same way, the medieval knights were expected to be completely loyal to their lord and their religion. Loyalty has always been a part of the warrior's code of honor. To turn your back on someone that you have given your friendship and loyalty to, is nothing more than an act of dishonor.

Of course, in today's society, the warrior is not required to be totally loyal to some Daimyo or lord. This is a good thing since it is so rare to actually find leaders of honor and character. This is not to say that Daimyos and lords weren't less than honorable - many were. The fact that many of these men were less than honorable speaks to how highly warriors esteemed loyalty. They remained loyal to their lord, even when the lord did not deserve their loyalty.

This fact once again reinforces the warrior's dedication to his own standards. Once the warrior swore his loyalty to his Daimyo or his lord, he kept his word, no matter how the other party behaved. He did not let the lord's lack of character cause him to break his word of honor. They took their oath seriously.

True warriors today are not bound by an oath to give their loyalty to anyone; it is given as a part of their code of honor. There are no laws which require you to be loyal to your friends or your family. Ada Velez-Boardley stated, "Loyalty is the pledge of truth to oneself and others." You and you alone, make a firm decision to be loyal. Sometimes it is hard to maintain your loyalty to those in your life, especially when they do not deserve your loyalty. But it is exactly at times like those, when they do not deserve your friendship, that your loyalty is tested. It is when people are acting like total jerks or when they make mistakes, that they most need your loyal friendship.

As I mentioned in a previous chapter, the warrior doesn't change his character because someone does or does not *deserve* his support. He lives his life by his own standards, despite the actions of others. Being loyal to someone does not mean that you always agree with his actions or that you even like him all the time. What it means is that you have made a firm decision and have given him your friendship and loyalty. Once you have done that, you should live up to your word.

This in no way means that you can never withdraw your loyalty from someone. You can give your friendship to someone, but if they utterly reject your friendship and your attempts to support them, you are not required to continue to support them. This is not the same as being disloyal. In this case, it is the other person's decision to end the friendship, not yours. The true warrior is the best friend that someone could possibly have, but if his friendship is rejected, he is released from any duty that he had to be a loyal friend.

While the warrior would never turn his back on a friend or be disloyal to a friend, he is certainly not required to put up with being treated in a disrespectful manner or to continue to extend the hand of friendship to someone who has made it clear that he doesn't want his friendship. This is totally different from the warrior being a disloyal friend. In this case his friendship is being thrown away by the other person and he no longer has any duty to be loyal or supportive to this person.

On the other hand, the opposite of this scenario should never happen. The superior man will never turn his back on his friend and end the friendship out of some unwarranted, selfish reasons. Once the warrior has entered into the sacred bond of true friendship, he will honor that friendship, as far as it depends on him. It is for this reason that the warrior should be carefully selective when it comes to forming true friendships, instead of mere acquaintances.

When you have decided to give your hand in friendship, you should remain loyal to your friend, even when your friend is in the wrong. This doesn't mean that you have to join him in his misguided actions or support everything that he does. Never lower your standards just to go along with something that someone else is doing, whether he is your friend or not. Being supportive and loyal doesn't mean you support everything that your friend does; it simply means that you *support* your friend. This is an important distinction.

Let's look at an example. Say your friend is having a very hard time financially and has made the very bad decision to sell illegal drugs in order to get enough money to pay his bills and keep his house. Of course you shouldn't support his decision, but this doesn't mean that you throw in the towel on the friendship. If this is a true friendship, you should support your friend by trying to counsel him about the error of his ways. You should try to stop him from making a possible life-changing mistake because of utter frustration over his finances.

This is in no way supporting his decision to sell drugs, rather it is you being a good friend and trying your best to support him through the bad time that he is going through. Whether or not he listens to you or takes your advice is not up to you; whether or not you remain a loyal, supportive friend is. See the difference? To quote Charles Dickens, "She was truest to them in the season of trial, as all the quietly loyal and good will always be."

Another analogy would be to look at the loyalty that a good dog has to his owner. If you have a good dog and have raised it from the time it was a puppy, trained it well, spent time with it, loved it, and made it a part of your life, it will certainly be loyal to you. Your devoted friend will love you and most likely even put his life on the line for you, depending on the breed. But even the most loyal dog will not follow his owner in certain acts of desperation.

For example, let's say that for some reason you became severely depressed and decided that you would commit suicide by hiking to the top of a cliff and jumping off. Your loyal companion would certainly hike up the mountain with you, giving you love and support all the way, and sensing something is wrong, he would probably give you even more of his attention throughout the hike. But when it comes down to you actually jumping off the cliff, he will not follow you off the edge. He would do what he could to alert someone to your death or to get someone to help, but he would not join you in your misguided action.

This is the same type of loyalty and support the true warrior should give to those in his life. He doesn't turn his back on them simply because they are wrong or misguided. Instead he does all that he can to help them and support them, but if they persist in destroying their life, he will not destroy his life as well.

This same principle applies to the first example where your friend has decided to sell drugs. You should support him the best you can, and not turn your back on him, but at the same time, you cannot join him in his desperate actions. There is a big difference between loving and supporting your friend, and allowing your friend to drag you down. I use this quote by Gracian often, and it bears repeating here, "The man of principle never forgets what he is, because of what others are."

There is a quote by Sir Francis Osborne that fits perfectly with this discussion, "In seeking to save another, beware of drowning yourself." Remain a loyal friend, but understand that all you can do is the best that you can do. You control your actions, but you can't always control the outcome. Be loyal and do what you can to help, but in the end you must realize that everyone has to make his own decisions. You can't control everything, no matter how much you would like to.

I have one last comment on my example about the friend who decides to sell drugs. You may be thinking that anyone who would sell drugs doesn't *deserve* your support and that you would be justified to immediately end this friendship. This is how most people would view this situation, but as with so many things, the true warrior looks at things a bit differently. Remember, *deserve* has nothing to do with it.

When you have given your hand in friendship, your duty requires you to exhaust every option before giving up. While others may see your friendship with this person as condoning his actions, you know better. Takuan Soho stated, "Each action of the warrior is performed from a place of fundamental wisdom…it is completely different from the ordinary behavior of a fool. Even if it looks the same, it is different on the inside."

Your loyalty to friends and family should have no limit, although it may be expressed in ways that others cannot understand. Don't worry how others view you; just act according to what you know is right where your loyalty is concerned.

Meditations on Loyalty

You don't earn loyalty in a day.
You earn loyalty day-by-day.
Jeffrey Gitomer

She was truest to them in the season of trial,
as all the quietly loyal and good will always be.
Charles Dickens.

Though bitter, good medicine cures illness.
Though it may hurt, loyal criticism
will have beneficial effects.
Sima Qian

One loyal friend is worth ten thousand relatives.
Euripides

Within the hearts of men, loyalty and consideration
are esteemed greater than success.
Bryant H. McGill

Confidentiality is a virtue of the loyal,
as loyalty is the virtue of faithfulness.
Edwin Louis Cole

If having a soul means being able to
feel love and loyalty and gratitude,
then animals are better off than a lot of humans.
James Herriot

You've got to give loyalty down,
if you want loyalty up.
Donald T. Regan

Loyalty and devotion lead to bravery.
Morihei Ueshiba

Your loyalty to friends and family should have no limit,
although it may be expressed in ways
that others cannot understand.
Bohdi Sanders

Loyalty to the country always.
Loyalty to the government when it deserves it.
Mark Twain

No more duty can be urged upon those
who are entering the great theater of life
than simple loyalty to their best convictions.
Edwin Hubbel Chapin

No one but yourself knows
whether you are cowardly and cruel,
or loyal and devout; others do not see you;
they surmise you by uncertain conjectures;
they perceive not so much your nature as your art.
Michel de Montaigne

Chapter 29

Total Self-Defense
The Warrior's Invincibility

Total Self-Defense: The use of reasonable force, mental intelligence, and other means, to defend yourself, your family, or your property against any tangible harm, whether physical, financial, or otherwise.

There is much more to self-defense than being able to defend yourself against a physical assault. Although self-defense has become synonymous with martial arts, in reality it encompasses many other aspects besides a physical attack. The true warrior is concerned with keeping himself and his family completely safe and secure, not just perfecting his martial arts skills.

As a warrior, you have a duty to protect your family, period. Your duty is not merely to protect your family from physical attacks, but from any danger which might threaten them. In today's world the threat of a physical assault is a very real, valid threat, but it isn't the only danger lurking in the shadows. In fact, defending yourself from a physical assault, even if you are proficient in your martial arts skills, carries with it hidden dangers that you may not have considered.

You have to be very careful when it comes to using your martial arts to defend yourself. Don't get me wrong, when your life is on the line you do whatever it takes to protect yourself and your family. That is a given. But what you must keep in mind is your overall objective, which is to protect yourself and your family. There is a right way and a wrong way to do everything, including defending yourself.

We live in a different world than we did 20 or 30 years ago. Today's society is plagued by political correctness and a lack of common sense. Every prison houses men and women who are there simply because they defended themselves against a predator's attack. While they may have successfully defended themselves against the predator that attacked them, they failed to protect themselves from our over-reaching, corrupt legal system.

Self-defense means self-defense, period. It leaves nothing out. Today, you not only have to defend yourself against predators and criminals, but you also have to defend yourself against the police, the government and the legal system. In the long run, our inept and corrupt legal system has done more damage to many people's lives than physical assaults, which were short of death, could have possibly done. This fact is sad but true. Self-defense today is much trickier than at any time in the history of our world.

The wise warrior will understand this fact and incorporate it into his self-defense training. Han Fei Tzu wrote, "As circumstances change, the ways of dealing with them alter too." Well, I've got news for you, in case you haven't noticed, circumstances have changed. It's a different world. We live in a society where employees can foil an armed robbery, possibly saving their lives, and the lives of others around them, and still be reprimanded and fired for their actions. We live in a society where an armed criminal can break into your home to rob and kill you, and if you shoot him and paralyze him, he can sue you for protecting yourself.

These facts clearly signify that our world has changed. The mental patients are now in charge of the asylum. There is an ancient Indian proverb which states, "If you live in the river you should make friends with the crocodile." You must understand *all* of the possible dangers that you could face in today's world, not merely the ones that you learn about in your martial arts class.

When you train for self-defense today, you have to consider dangers such as corrupt police, court costs, law suits, and even going to jail. These are all very real dangers for you and your family. Our legal system is no longer a system which weighs what is just. It has become a monstrous bureaucracy which is all about making money. True justice is a thing of the past. If you get hauled into court, your life is on the line and it is a crap shoot. Even if you are in the right and are acquitted, it will still cost you thousands of dollars in lawyer fees to defend yourself.

The wise warrior needs to consider these things. Do some research on how our system really works. Learn what the police and courts looks for that indicates that you acted in self-defense and that your actions were justified. Research, not only how criminals and predators think, but also how the police think and how their system works. What you find will be scary and will make you think differently about self-defense.

There are several enlightening books on the market which give you insight into how to successfully deal with the police. I can tell you straight up that you shouldn't trust the police to protect you or your rights; don't place your safety or the safety of your family in anyone's hands but your own. Understand that most people don't care about you.

It is up to you to make sure that you and your family are safe – in every way. This is what total self-defense is all about. The word "total" leaves nothing out. Self-defense shouldn't simply focus only on one type of threat. If there are several kinds of danger lurking in your path and you only train to address one of those kinds of danger, are you truly prepared to protect yourself or your family? Think about that. You have to know your rights and how the system works.

Our system of government is corrupt and it has been for many, many years, but it is getting worse. It is easy for the warrior to focus on martial arts, meditation, and physical fitness. These are things that he finds interesting, fun, and exciting to practice and explore. But your duty extends much further than martial arts training. You have to consider many other factors when it comes to keeping your family safe, and some of these will not be as exciting, interesting or fun as studying martial arts.

Politicians and government bureaucrats can turn your life into a nightmare and utterly destroy you as easily as some thug in a back alley. A criminal is a criminal; they merely differ in their approach. Total self-defense has to incorporate a vast array of knowledge. You need to educate yourself concerning the financial world as well as the criminal justice system. The IRS can turn your family upside down with a simple audit, even if you have tried your best to conform to their laws and regulations.

By now you should be starting to understand that there is much more involved in keeping your family safe, than simply knowing how to fight and defend yourself physically, and even in the physical arena there are many other aspects to consider. One important part of total self-defense, as far as your physical/mental skills are concerned, is learning de-escalation techniques. This is a vital part of total self-defense, especially if there are witnesses around you at the time of the conflict. Let's looks at an example.

If you are in a bar and some ruffian decides to target you, you shouldn't just use him for a punching bag to teach him a lesson. This could cause you a lot of trouble. What you want to do is to do everything in your power to de-escalate the situation, while making sure that the many witnesses in the bar can clearly see that you don't want to fight, and are trying your best to settle things peaceably. You do this with your dialog, your gestures, the tone of your voice, etc. And you should do this sincerely; you should *truly* not want to fight if you can avoid it.

You do this for two reasons. First, you do it because it is the right thing to do. You never want to hurt someone if you can avoid it. Second, you are covering your butt. If things do come to blows, you will have a room full of witnesses that will testify that you didn't want to fight and that you tried your best to walk away peaceably, but were *forced* to defend yourself. As Baltasar Gracian stated, "Let cold deliberation take the place of sudden outburst."

Of course you don't always have the chance to de-escalate things. If someone walks up and tries to take a cheap shot at you, for whatever reason, you have to react immediately. I am not talking about a situation like that. That is a totally different kind of situation. But, if you have a chance to de-escalate things, do so. Don't let your pride or emotions cause you more problems. Think rationally and remember your objective, which is to keep yourself and your family safe.

Self-defense is not about pride or proving how tough you are. It is about one thing and one thing only, keeping yourself and your family safe – in every way. If you want to prove how tough you are, enter some full-contact fighting contest. Don't try to prove how tough you are in a situation that may cost you and your family financially, emotionally, and physically. Putting some idiot in his place may feel good temporarily, but that good feeling will soon turn to regret if it costs you thousands of dollars and several years in prison.

I am just skimming the surface, concerning this topic. There are many, many other topics where the issue of total self-defense should be considered by the wise man. Things such as your choice of friends, drinking too much in public, drug use, home protection, speaking your mind in the workplace, etcetera, all can jeopardize, in one way or another, the overall safety of you and your family, and should be taken into consideration as part of your overall self-defense.

Another aspect of total self-defense is that of being prepared for emergencies. You should have emergency plans for your family in case of natural disasters such as fires, floods, tornadoes, etc. In addition, you should also be prepared for the consequences of other kinds of disasters that could disrupt your food supply, your access to clean water, the power to your home, or fuel for your vehicles. These are all things that most people take for granted, but these are all very real threats.

There are many books out there which give you a lot of information on the many different aspects of survival, and I highly recommend that you find a good one and do some research on the subject. You don't wait until you are assaulted to start thinking about your martial arts skills, and you shouldn't wait until your house is on fire to think about what steps to take to get your family out safely. Take the time to prepare in advance. Total self-defense incorporates all of this plus martial arts training as well.

Martial arts training is definitely a part of the warrior lifestyle and, in my opinion, should be a part of everybody's life in today's society. Everyone needs to know, at least some basic self-defense strategies and techniques. There are a lot of really bad people in this world, and it is a part of preparedness to know how these people think and how to keep yourself safe from the many predators that roam our streets and neighborhoods.

Many people wrongfully see martial arts as teaching violence or all about fighting. This is not the case. Depending on the style and the instructor, martial arts teach much of what I discuss in *Modern Bushido*. But, like I said, it depends on the instructor and the style. It can be difficult to find a martial arts dojo that teaches both character training and actual, *useful* self-defense techniques in the same class, or in some cases, at all.

There are many kinds of martial arts and each have their own techniques, philosophy, and overall views of what martial arts should be. Some are merely interested in sports or tournament applications, and others only focus on mixed martial arts competitions. Others are mainly teaching an ancient art form. While each of these have their place, and there is nothing inherently wrong with any of them, in my opinion, the true warrior should focus his attention on a martial art which teaches real-life applications – true, usable self-defense.

What I mean by *usable self-defense* is a martial art that teaches you techniques and strategies that will keep you safe on the street. Learning a martial art for the sake of learning an art is fine. These martial arts teach the art of ancient weapons, katas, and pre-prescribed techniques. This is very interesting and fun to learn, but a lot of what is taught in these type classes is not really useful on the streets for personal self-defense.

For example, how many people are going to be walking the streets carrying a sword or a naginata? Learning such things is mainly for entertainment, tournaments, or just plain fun. For actual self-defense applications I believe that the true warrior needs to concentrate more on realistic martial arts training. This kind of training teaches real-life applications and prepares the student for what he is most likely to run into in today's world.

Realistic self-defense classes are more interested in teaching techniques which truly work, as opposed to teaching traditional techniques. Don't get me wrong, I am definitely not saying that traditional techniques don't work. My black belt is in Shotokan, a traditional style of karate. What I am suggesting is that it is fine to learn traditional martial arts styles, but you will want to spend some time training in some modern, realistic martial arts as well.

No matter what style of martial arts you decide is best for you, you will want to make sure that it addresses three major areas: self-defense techniques, de-escalation techniques, and mental preparedness. Of course a good martial arts instructor is going to teach you much more than just these three skill sets, but you want to make sure that you find someone who is, at a minimum, an expert in these three. Let's look at each of these three areas of self-defense.

First, it should go without saying that any martial arts training should teach you good self-defense techniques. These include things such as punches, kicks, joint locks, pressure points, and using different weapons, just to name a few. These techniques should be uncomplicated and easy to learn. For realistic self-defense, you don't need to know how to do some jumping, spinning roundhouse kick. If someone tries to sell you on using something like that for self-defense, he does not know what he is talking about and you should find a different instructor.

When it comes to personal self-defense, you want to learn simple, useable techniques, not fancy Hollywood stunts. Also, learning to use traditional weapons is of little use, as far as self-defense applications are concerned. It is much more useful for you to learn how to use modern weapons such as firearms and knives. The one exception to this rule is learning how to fight with a staff. There are many times when you could have access to a makeshift staff in today's world, so knowing how to use anything from a bo staff to a hanbo would be useful training, and classified under "good to know."

In addition, a good self-defense class will include lessons on the anatomy of the human body. The more you know about the human body and how it is designed, the better able you are to understand how to take it apart. You need to know how the different joints work, where pressure points are located, which areas to attack and which not to, and which spots are dangerous and could kill someone. This is all a part of learning about the physical aspect of self-defense.

The second area that any good martial arts instructor should teach you is de-escalation techniques. I touched on de-escalation techniques earlier in this chapter, but it is an important subject, so I will expand on it more here. De-escalation techniques basically teach the student how to put out a fire before it starts. The applications of these techniques are many, but they aren't taught in many dojos today.

Too many martial arts instructors only teach students how to kick and punch, basically, how to fight. This is shortsighted instruction. Sun Tzu wrote, "To subdue an enemy without fighting is the greatest of skills." This is what de-escalation techniques are all about – winning without fighting. If your instructor does not teach de-escalation techniques, and give you ample time to practice these techniques in real-life scenario training, you should either find a new instructor or get some independent training. Yes, it is this important!

A vital part of de-escalation training is understanding how predators think and how their minds work. My book, *Wicked Wisdom: Explorations into the Dark Side*, is a good source for this information. It delves into how criminals and predators think, and also gives you a lot of information about de-escalation techniques. If you understand how these people think, it is much easier to understand how to deal with them. Like George Washington said, "To be prepared for war is one of the most effective means of preserving peace."

The last area of any good martial arts instruction is mental preparedness. This area is closely related to learning de-escalation techniques. In fact, they can be seen as overlapping. Mental preparedness is a major part of realistic martial arts training. You can know every technique perfectly, but if your mind panics when someone attacks you, your techniques are almost worthless. This is where mental preparedness comes into play. You have to learn how to control your mind in high-stress, high-adrenaline situations.

It is one thing to spar with a friendly partner, in a safe and controlled setting, but it is another thing altogether when you are assaulted by a muscle-bound thug who truly wants to hurt you. You have to learn how to remain calm and rational in these kinds of situations. Realistic martial art training teaches you this skill.

Learning how to successfully defend your family should not be seen as an option to the warrior – it is one of your main duties. It is for this reason that I think it is much more important to learn modern, realistic martial arts techniques, than to study traditional arts. I also think that every warrior should learn to not only use modern weapons, but to become proficient in their use during self-defense situations.

Again, I am not against learning traditional martial arts styles. If you are interested in traditional martial arts, by all means take classes and learn what you are interested in learning. All I am trying to get across to you is that if you do decide to learn traditional martial arts, you should supplement that training with some realistic training as well. In fact, the more you learn, the better off you will be, as far as your own personal self-defense is concerned. You can never have too much knowledge.

There is a Native American saying which states, "The hunter can make many mistakes, the hunted, only one." Predators are the hunters. They can makes many mistakes and still live to try again, unless one of their mistakes lands them in jail or dead. You, on the other hand, are the hunted. You can't afford to make a mistake if you are attacked by one of these predators. Being unprepared or untrained could mean death for you, if your path crosses paths with a dangerous predator.

It is for this reason that you should take your martial arts training, and your overall total self-defense skills, seriously. You should look at your martial arts training as a matter of life or death, not simply as another fun activity that you participate in two or three times a week. You have to be as prepared as possible for whatever the winds of life blow your way. Good, realistic, martial art training is a huge part of being prepared.

This chapter is just a very quick summary on the subject of total self-defense. There are many books dedicated to this subject and I would highly recommend that you do some research on each of the various aspects of total self-defense preparedness. It is always better to be over prepared for the unexpected, than it is to find yourself facing a bad situation which you are not prepared to handle.

Total self-defense means that you are capable of defending yourself against whatever may threaten your life, or your way of life. This topic encompasses a wide variety of situations, far too many to be covered in this short chapter. It will serve you well to prepare yourself as well as you possibly can for the possible dangers that you could face. Remember the ancient saying, "Only a warrior chooses pacifism; others are condemned to it." Give yourself the choice.

Meditations on Total Self-Defense

What is of supreme importance in war
is to attack the enemy's strategy.
Sun Tzu

What folly is it to play a game in which you
can lose incomparably more than you can win.
Francesco Guicciardini

He who lacks foresight and underestimates
his enemy will surely be captured by him.
Sun Tzu

You have everything to gain
from managing your affairs secretly.
Francesco Guicciardini

Let cold deliberation take the place of sudden outburst.
Baltasar Gracian

Silence is the safest policy if you are unsure of yourself.
La Rochefoucauld

If a battle cannot be won, do not fight it.
Sun Tzu

Don't spit in the well: you'll be thirsty by and by.
Russian Proverb

As circumstances change,
the ways of dealing with them alter too.
Han Fei Tzu

Every man counts as an enemy,
but not every man as a friend.
Very few can do us good, but nearly all, harm.
Baltasar Gracian

Men are so false, so insidious, so deceitful and
cunning in their wiles, so avid in their own interest,
and so oblivious to other's interest, that you cannot
go wrong if you believe little and trust less.
Francesco Guicciardini

If you live in the river you should
make friends with the crocodile.
Indian Proverb

Prepare yourself in good fortune for the bad.
Baltasar Gracian

It is the foolish sheep that makes the wolf its confessor.
Italian Proverb

If you have doubts about someone,
your true and best security consists in having things
so arranged that he cannot hurt you even if he wants to.
Francesco Guicciardini

Embrace the snake and it will bite you.
Bulgarian Proverb

In seeking to save another, beware of drowning yourself.
Sir Francis Osborne

Never get angry except on purpose.
Japanese Maxim

More Meditations on Total Self-Defense

Strength is defeated by strategy.
Philippine Proverb

To subdue an enemy without
fighting is the greatest of skills.
Sun Tzu

You must be deadly serious in training.
Gichin Funakoshi

Avoiding danger is not cowardice.
Philippine Proverb

To be prepared for war is one of the
most effective means of preserving peace.
George Washington

He does not guard himself well
who is not always on his guard.
French Proverb

The good fighters of old first put themselves beyond
the possibility of defeat, and then waited for
an opportunity of defeating the enemy.
Sun Tzu

It is usually the reply that causes the fight.
Japanese Proverb

Victory is not gained through idleness.
German Proverb

Rely not on the likelihood of the enemy's not coming,
but on our own readiness to receive him;
not on the chance of his not attacking, but rather
on the fact that we have made our position unassailable.
Sun Tzu

Make yourself a sheep, and the wolf is ready.
Russian Proverb

The hunter can make many mistakes,
the hunted, only one.
Native American Maxim

In peace do not forget war.
Japanese Proverb

Tomorrow's battle is won during today's practice.
Samurai Maxim

Even in the sheath the knife must be sharp.
Finnish Proverb

Invincibility depends on one's self;
the enemy's vulnerability on him.
Sun Tzu

Chapter 30

Acceptance
Living in the Shadow of Death

Acceptance: The realization of a fact or truth and the process of coming to terms with it

Robert Louis Stevenson wrote, "Old and young, we are all on our last cruise." Warriors must accept the fact that at some point, they are going to die. The Samurai reflected on their death daily. This practice helped keep them focused on the things in their life which really mattered and served to remind them that every day is a special gift to be lived to the fullest. As Dhaggi Ramanashi wrote, and was quoted in the great warrior epic, *Braveheart*, "Everybody who lives dies. But not everybody who dies has lived."

Marcus Aurelius expressed this same thought stating, "It is not death that a man should fear, he should fear never beginning to live." And Dag Hammarskjold echoed this sentiment stating, "Do not seek death. Death will find you. But seek the road which makes death a fulfillment." This is an excellent quote for the warrior – seek the road which makes death a fulfillment. This actually sums up the warrior lifestyle, for it is the road which makes death a fulfillment.

Everyone should live life to the fullest and strive to get as much out of each and every day as humanly possible. Nobody knows when death will suddenly appear at his door, so it is short-sided and foolish not to live each day to the fullest. This doesn't just mean being as active as possible in order to get as much done as you possibly can before you die. As I said before, you have to balance the three parts of your life – the spiritual, the mental, and the physical.

Nobody knows how much time they have to live on this earth. Even if you weren't trying to live a life of excellence, this fact alone should be enough to cause you to keep your affairs in order and live life to the fullest. The reason so many people don't live their life this way is because they refuse to think about the uncertainty of life. For many, it is a depressing thought. It wouldn't be that way if they would spend some time reflecting on their spirituality.

Without being clear about your spiritual beliefs or giving any thought to spiritual things at all, death is definitely a scary, depressing thought. You can only be at peace with the fact that your time is limited if you spend some time meditating on your spirituality and come to peace with your beliefs concerning God and your relationship with God. Once you have reached this point and know what you believe and why, you will find that you are more at peace with the subject of death and living your life to the fullest here and now.

Warriors of old spent time reflecting on their spiritual beliefs because they never knew when doing their duty would result in their death. Modern warriors should follow their lead and make sure that they are at peace in their spiritual life. Part of being prepared is being prepared for the possibility of death. Charles Simmons wrote, "Every person ought daily to reflect upon the uncertainty of life, and the consequences of sudden death." This is true. The Samurai knew this, the sages knew this, and you should know this too.

Thinking of the consequences of death doesn't have to be a morbid, depressing process. Rather than thinking about how terrible or sad it will be, think about it from the viewpoint of life is short, so you must make every moment count. Use the fact that time goes by fast and your time on this earth will be over faster than you can imagine, to motivate yourself to live your life to the fullest. Spend time with your friends and family. Make sure you keep your affairs in order. Live your life; don't just eat, sleep and work.

The sands in your hour glass will flow at the same rate whether you live life to the fullest or just go through the motions. Sai Baba illustrated this very well in the following analogy, "When you are intent upon a journey, after you purchase your ticket and board the train – whether you sit quietly, lie down, read or meditate, the train will take you to the destination. So, too, at birth each living thing has received a ticket to the event of death and is now on the journey."

The sand in your hour glass is like the train in this analogy. It will continue to flow, at the same rate, towards the time of your death no matter what you do during that time. The sands of time are not affected by how you spend your time. It doesn't matter if you sleep, workout, work to improve yourself, live with a positive outlook, or waste your life in a drug induced fog, your time continues to flow (that is, unless you do something like throw your hour glass off the top of a building and bring about your own death).

It is up to you to decide how you will live your life. You decide how your limited time on this earth will be spent. Don't fear death or waste your time putting off living until sometime in the future – live your life now! Distich Moralia stated, "Give up fearing death; it's at all times foolish to miss life's pleasures for fear of death." If you are putting off enjoying your life in the present, and instead you are thinking that you will start enjoying your life after you accomplish this or after you make enough money, etc., you are making a big mistake.

This kind of thinking is a trap. There will always be another reason to put off living and enjoying your life in the present – no money, a big project, etc. This list could go on and on. You must live while you are living. You can still take care of all the menial things that we all have in our lives, while at the same time, living your life to the fullest. Living is living. You don't have to compartmentalize your life. It is okay to enjoy your life and take time to smell the roses, even while you are struggling to make your way in this world.

Shinso stated, "No matter what road I travel, I am going home." Don't take everything so seriously that it subtracts from your enjoyment of living your life. Although you can't control the sands of time, you do control how you live your life while those grains of sand are flowing through the hour glass. Accepting the fact that the days of your life are numbered shouldn't take away from your excitement or enjoyment of life; this is not why the warrior meditates on his death.

Meditating on death is merely a way to keep you focused on living life to the fullest. If you think about the fact that you do not have all the time in the world and that you are getting older every day, you will be more motivated to live your life now, instead of putting off living until later. If there are things that you want to do during your lifetime, do them now. Don't put off living until sometime in the future.

The other benefit is that when you understand that there are no guarantees concerning how long you have to live on this earth, you will be motivated to make every moment count with your friends and family. This uncertainty should motivate you to keep your affairs in order so your family is provided for in the event of your unexpected death.

This is exactly why the Samurai spent time daily contemplating their death. They knew that their life was especially uncertain because of the customs of their lifestyle. They could be commanded to commit suicide at any time by their Lord, and they would obey, no questions asked. In addition, there was also the very real chance of having to fight to the death for self-defense or in a duel. They had to keep their affairs in order and be prepared for death at any moment.

You, on the other hand, are not beholding to anyone who may command you to commit suicide, but your life is no more guaranteed than that of the Samurai of old. In fact, your life is just as uncertain. You never know when you will be in a fatal car wreck, some freak accident, or caught up in some act of terrorism. It is just as important for you to have your affairs in order and to be prepared to meet your Maker as it was for the Samurai warriors. Like Cicero said, "No man can be ignorant that he must die, nor be sure that he may not this very day."

Even a long life, is short. Before you know it, you will wake up and see new lines on your face and your body will start to feel old, and you will think that just yesterday you were young. The years definitely go by fast. Time is very deceptive in this way. Juvenal stated, "The short bloom of our brief and narrow life flies fast away. While we are calling for flowers and wine and women, old age is upon us." Homer echoed this sentiment stating, "Men flourish only for a moment."

However, reflecting on how short your life may be is no excuse for living recklessly or irresponsibly. This is a mistake that some people make when they start to meditate on how short life actually is. They mistake living life to the fullest, for living life selfishly and recklessly. Bias tells us that, "We should live life as though our life would be both long and short."

You aren't on this earth to simply exist, but rather to live, and live well. After all, you aren't alive if you aren't living. Your life is going to be what you make it. As Christian Furchtegott Gellert wrote, "Live as you will wish to have lived when you are dying." Live your life with no regrets. Of course everyone is going to have some regrets, but you should do your best to live so that you don't regret having wasted your allotted time during this life.

Kok Yim Ci Yuen said, "The greatest gratification is embodied in the knowledge on one's deathbed that one has no regrets from his or her life, and that one has spent one's days with a sincere and harmonious attitude." Accepting your mortality doesn't mean moping around waiting for death to take you away; it means understanding that life is a gift and that you must use that gift before it is too late. I will end this chapter with a quote from Cervantes, it is actually Don Quixote's Creed, and a good philosophy of life, "Take a deep breath of life and consider how it should be lived."

Meditations on Acceptance

Old and young, we are all on our last cruise.
Robert Louis Stevenson

When you are intent upon a journey, after you purchase
your ticket and board the train – whether you sit quietly,
lie down, read or meditate, the train will take you to the
destination. So, too, at birth each living thing has received
a ticket to the event of death and is now on the journey.
Sai Baba

Take a deep breath of life and
consider how it should be lived.
Don Quixote's Creed

None dies except in appearance. In fact what is called birth
is the passage from essence to substance, and what is called
death is on the contrary the passage from substance to
essence. Nothing is born and nothing dies in reality,
but all first appears and then becomes invisible.
Apollonius of Tyana

So live your life that the fear of death
can never enter your heart.
Tecumseh

The proper function of man is to live, not to exist.
I will not waste my days in trying to prolong them.
Jack London

Do you not know that disease and death must overtake us,
no matter what we are doing?...What do you wish to be
doing when it overtakes you?...If you have anything better to
be doing when you are so overtaken, get to work on that.
Epictetus

It is not death that a man should fear,
he should fear never beginning to live.
Marcus Aurelius

Live as you will wish to have lived when you are dying.
Christian Furchtegott Gellert

We should live as though our life
would be both long and short.
Bias

Do not seek death. Death will find you.
But seek the road which makes death a fulfillment.
Dag Hammarskjold

Every person ought daily to reflect
upon the uncertainty of life, and
the consequences of sudden death.
Charles Simmons

Everybody who lives dies.
But not everybody who dies has lived.
Dhaggi Ramanashi

Chapter 31

The Fool
The Antithesis of the Warrior

Fool: Somebody considered lacking a good sense of judgment; an unintelligent person; a ridiculous person.

I have devoted quite a bit of time discussing the traits of the true warrior, but sometimes it is helpful to our understanding to see the opposite side of the coin – the traits of the fool. The actions of the fool are usually the opposite of those of the true warrior. Someone who is a fool is considered to be somebody who lacks good sense or good judgment. He lacks the character traits of the superior man, and he embraces many traits which the warrior strives to eliminate from his life.

The foolish man doesn't quite comprehend the law of karma. The law of karma is the total effect of a person's actions and conduct during his life. Karma is basically the law of reciprocity. This means that whatever you do comes back to you in one form or another. The unwise man doesn't understand this, and thus wonders why he continually has bad luck throughout his lifetime.

He fosters the internal enemies – feelings of anger, hate, revenge, greed, jealousy, malice, and prejudice, without ever stopping to think about whether his way of life is right or wrong. The concept of right and wrong can never become fully established in his life because it is constantly being overshadowed by selfish thoughts of comfort, desires and profit. Justice takes a back seat to his own comfort or selfish desires. The book of *Proverbs* puts it well, stating, "Like snow in summer or rain in harvest, honor is not fitting for a fool."

Although this type of man doesn't deserve true honor, he often plays the role of the charlatan, claiming honors and titles for himself which he doesn't deserve. John Crowne does a good job of telling us why this is so, stating, "A fool, indeed, has great need of a title; it teaches men to call him count or duke, and thus forget his proper name of fool." How often do we see this in today's world! Just think of the corrupt, unethical politician who is always called the "Honorable Mr. Jones." Honorable indeed! Sakya Pandit taught, "Though a wicked man appears good in his conduct, it is but hypocrisy." How well this applies to many of our politicians and leaders!

Every human being feels emotions such as anger or hate at one time or another, but the foolish man harbors these feelings and nourishes them, until they many times manifest in inappropriate and low actions. Fools are rash and allow their emotions to guide their actions, never stopping to consider that their emotions are irrational or that their actions will have lasting consequences for them down the road. Baltasar Gracian wrote, "Fools always rush in, for all fools are rash." Rash actions are rarely wise, rational decisions. The foolish man never stops to consider this fact, as rational thought is a foreign concept to him the majority of the time.

Although his thoughts and actions are many times shameful, his pride is without limits. Alexander Pope wrote, "Pride is the never-failing vice of fools, and this point has proven to be true throughout the ages." No matter how undeserving of honor or honors, the fool's pride never wavers. He thinks of himself way more highly than he should, while at the same time looking at the true man of honor with contempt.

The idea of emulating the wise man, or the warrior lifestyle, never crosses his mind, with the exception of doing so for some ulterior, dishonorable purpose. He is not interested in truly being a man of honor, but rather in *appearing* to be a man of honor in order to increase his profits or position. To him, this is what passes as wisdom. The concept of holding himself to a higher standard because of his principles is sheer lunacy in his eyes.

He cannot perceive the benefit of holding himself to a higher standard if it doesn't increase his bottom line in some way. He sees the true man of honor as the fool because he simply doesn't have the capacity to understand the true meaning of honor. William Blake wrote, "A fool sees not the same tree that a wise man sees." How true this is!

There is a Chinese proverb that states, "Summer insects are not equipped to talk about ice; a frog in a well is not equipped to discuss the ocean." In the same way, the fool cannot comprehend the warrior lifestyle. He has no concept of the many traits discussed in *Modern Bushido*; they are simply foreign concepts to him. Confucius made this point perfectly saying, "The superior man stands in awe of the words of the sages. The inferior man does not stand in awe of them; he is disrespectful to important people; he mocks the words of the sages."

He mocks the very teachings that would help him transform his life. There is very little wisdom found in him at all, yet he talks as if he is the most intelligent man on the planet. This inferior man revels in hearing his own opinions and always has to interject his two cents worth into every conversation. Benjamin Franklin stated, "Half wits talk much but say little," thus describing the foolish man perfectly.

Plato taught us that, "Wise men talk because they have something to say; fools because they have to say something." The sages throughout the ages have echoed this very sentiment about the inferior man. The book of *Proverbs* states, "A fool finds no pleasure in understanding but delights in airing his own opinions." And Chuang Tzu taught, "Fools regard themselves as already awake." They think they are smarter than other people.

You will find that many of the fool's opinions are generalizations, and as William Blake stated, "To generalize is to be an idiot." It is by his own words that the fool reveals himself. Aesop taught us that, "Clothes may disguise a fool, but his words will give him away." Aesop went on to say, "The smaller the mind the greater the conceit." As you can clearly see, the inferior man doesn't give much thought to his words, he merely spouts whatever thoughts cross his mind, and they reveal him to be what he really is – a fool.

The *Bhagavad Gita* teaches us that, "Hypocrisy, arrogance, vanity, anger, harshness, ignorance; these characterize a man with foolish traits." These are obviously all traits which are completely opposite of the noble traits that the true warrior strives to develop in his life. The foolish man embraces these traits with the same vigor and passion as the warrior embraces the character traits discussed in *Modern Bushido*.

The Buddhist monk Bodhidharma stated, "Good and bad are distinct. Cause and effect are clear...But fools do not believe and fall straight into a hell of endless darkness without even knowing it...They are like blind people who do not believe there is such a thing as light. Even if you explain it to them, they still do not believe, because they are blind." It is basically impossible to explain the warrior lifestyle to the inferior man; he simply can't understand why anyone would live in such a way.

Nagarjuna stated, "Counsel given to fools excites but does not pacify. He who pours milk for a snake is only increasing its venom." Even if you do try to teach the way of the warrior to the fool, he will not change his lifestyle. Oh, he may get all excited about what you say and act as if he is going to change his life, but he rarely changes his true colors.

There is an ancient Irish proverb which states, "Don't give cherries to a pig; don't give advice to a fool." The reason for this is that it is a waste of your wisdom; fools rarely will act on good advice, choosing instead to go their own way, no matter how misguided that may be. It is best to hope that the fool learns from his own mistakes, although this too is rarely the case. As the Dayak proverb states, "No amount of rosewater can give a crow white feathers."

This outlook towards the fool is universally found throughout the world. In Japan they say, "There is no medicine to cure a fool." In China, the saying is, "Rotten wood cannot be carved." No matter how you put it, the meaning is the same: fools will not listen to sound advice.

Dr. Frank Crane wrote, "Every generation a new crop of fools comes on. They think they can beat the orderly universe. They conceive themselves to be above the eternal laws. They snatch good from Nature's store, and run...And one by one they all come back to Nature's counter, and pay – pay in tears, in agony, in despair; pay as fools before them have paid...Nature keeps books pitilessly. Your credit with her is good, but she collects; there is no land you can flee to and escape her bailiffs...She never forgets; she sees to it that you pay her every cent you owe, with interest."

This is a sad, but true commentary on the foolish man. He has all the same wisdom available to him as other men, but ignores it, choosing instead to go his own misguided way. He perceives himself to be different than all of those who went before him, and pays no heed to the wisdom of the elders. This man is not capable of learning from the past, but instead only has the capability to learn by making his own mistakes, many of which are permanent.

These men are hotheaded and reckless. To teach the fool the martial arts, is to create a dangerous menace to society, as he uses what he knows only for his own personal gain, without regard to anyone else. The masters knew this fact and refused to teach martial arts to men of low character, but things are different in today's society. Today, everything appears to revolve around money.

As you can plainly see, the fool is indeed the antithesis of the warrior. The warrior lifestyle is something that he could never fully comprehend. It is a way of life that he could never live. Strive to live as a wise man and leave the characteristics of the fool behind and be a man of true honor and integrity.

Meditations on the Antithesis of the Warrior

And the burnt fool's bandaged finger
goes wobbling back to the fire.
Rudyard Kipling

It is the peculiar quality of a fool
to perceive the faults of others and to forget his own.
Cicero

The superior man stands in awe of the words of the sages.
The inferior man does not stand in awe of them:
he is disrespectful to important people;
he mocks the words of the sages.
Confucius

Stupidity always goes to extremes.
Baltasar Gracian

A fool sees not the same tree that a wise man sees.
William Blake

Whatever benefit one may give,
the wicked man is never grateful.
Nagarjuna

Fools have been and always will be the majority of mankind.
Denis Diderot

Any man can make mistakes,
but only an idiot persists in his error.
Cicero

Wise men talk because they have something to say;
fools because they have to say something.
Plato

Those who do not study are simply cattle in clothing.
Chinese Proverb

The recipe for perpetual ignorance is:
be satisfied with your opinions and
content with your knowledge.
Elbert Hubbard

To generalize is to be an idiot.
William Blake

Outside noisy, inside empty.
Chinese Proverb

The foolish person seeks happiness in the distance.
James Oppenheim

A fool will soon use up his money.
Japanese Proverb

A wise man guides his own course of action;
the fool follows another's direction.
Sakya Pandit

Conclusion

I hope that you have found this book to be a useful aid in your quest to live a life of excellence. In order for the character traits discussed in *Modern Bushido* to be useful in your life, you will have to make them a real part of your life. It does no good to merely read about these traits, mentally agree that you should integrate them into your daily life, and then forget about them. You have to internalize the traits for them to make any difference in your life.

As the Dhammapada states, "It is you who must make the effort; the sages can only teach." I am not saying that I am a sage in any sense of the word, but you have been given a lot of information from many different sages in this book. Now it is up to you to decide whether or not you want to take the teachings of these sages and make them a part of your life or whether you want to continue with your life as is. Only you can make this decision. Buddha taught, "No matter how many good words you read and speak of, what good will they do you if you do not put them into practice and use them?" Think about this.

Put the information that you have read in this book to use in your life. Put it to the test and see if it isn't a better way to live. Nobility is an attitude not a birthright. You decide whether or not you will live a noble life. You decide whether or not you will live the warrior lifestyle. You, and you alone, decide whether or not you will live a life of honor and will be a true warrior.

"One must make the warrior walk his everyday walk."
Miyamoto Musashi

~ Live With Honor ~

Bohdi Sanders, PhD

Modern Bushido
Living a Life of Excellence

Bohdi Sanders, PhD

Index

F

G

H

R

Ralph Bunche, 94
Ralph Marston, 181, 186
Ralph Waldo Trine, 26
Ramakrishna, 50, 138, 141
Relationships, 44
Rene G. Torres, 69
reputation, 1, 2, 4, 5, 6, 15, 19, 34, 45, 57, 80, 135, 182, 184
resentment, 29
respect, v, viii, 58, 65, 66, 67, 68, 69, 70, 74, 75, 78, 80, 106, 108, 109, 131, 132, 133, 160, 161, 168, 169, 170, 172, 173, 174
Respect, iii, 65, 66, 67, 69, 70
responsibility, 2, 10, 58, 99, 167, 168
revenge, 29, 44, 211
Rhonda Byrne, 26
Right Actions, iii, 33, 39
right and wrong, 11, 12, 13, 14, 57, 58, 59, 60, 62, 100, 101, 102, 211
Righteousness, 82
Robert Burton, 170, 174
Robert Crowley, 123
Robert L. Humphrey, 22
Robert Louis Stevenson, 89, 91, 205, 209
Robert Wood, 60
Romain Rolland, 7
Rudyard Kipling, 215
Rumi, 53, 56, 152

S

sages, 3, 18, 25, 54, 55, 56, 138, 151, 152, 158, 159, 206, 213, 215, 217
Sai Baba, 17, 28, 53, 56, 127, 129, 141, 145, 148, 168, 173, 206, 209
Saint Theresa, 90
Saint Thomas Aquinas, 23
Sakya Pandit, 50, 212, 216
Samuel Coleridge, 61, 63
Samuel Johnson, 16, 44, 79, 83
Samuel Richardson, 15
Samuel Smiles, 56
Samurai, v, 113, 124, 187, 204, 205, 206, 207, 208
Scott Adams, 127, 130
self-confidence, 74, 88, 106
self-defense, vii, viii, 22, 36, 37, 95, 114, 122, 152, 158, 193, 194, 195, 196, 197, 198, 200, 208
self-discipline, 72, 73, 74
self-esteem, 74, 171, 172
Self-knowledge, 112, 113
Self-Knowledge, iii, 111, 115
self-reflection, 53, 54
self-reliance, 156, 157, 158
Self-reliance, 155
Self-Reliance, iv, 155, 159
self-sufficient, 158, 171
Seneca, 24, 54, 64, 129
seven virtues, viii
Shakespeare, 45, 90, 91, 113, 115
Sheikh Muzaffer, 36
Shinso, 207
Shotokan, ii, 1, 125, 198
Sima Qian, 191
sincere, i, 5, 6, 19, 36, 42, 45, 46, 66, 77, 78, 100, 105, 106, 107, 108, 110, 208
sincerity, 77, 106, 107, 108, 109, 110, 134
Sincerity, iii, 105, 107, 109, 110
Sir Francis Osborne, 128, 190, 202
Sir John Vanbrugh, 132, 136
Socrates, 62, 64, 97, 99, 100, 101, 103, 112, 115, 116, 138, 141, 161, 163, 165
Sophocles, 3, 103
speech, 20, 41, 42, 43, 44, 45, 46, 47, 48, 151
spirit, ix, 1, 20, 23, 35, 71, 106, 117, 121, 132, 134, 137, 138, 139, 140, 141, 148, 151, 152, 153, 155, 157, 175, 177, 178
spiritual beliefs, 137, 140, 206
Spirituality, iii, 137, 139, 141
standards, vii, 2, 3, 4, 5, 9, 10, 11, 13, 14, 68, 71, 89, 95, 99, 128, 131, 132, 188, 189
stress, 44, 118, 119, 120, 128, 144, 146, 156, 199
Sun Tzu, 114, 122, 123, 154, 199, 201, 203, 204
superior man, vii, 1, 2, 3, 4, 5, 6, 8, 10, 11, 12, 16, 20, 23, 31, 38, 41, 45, 47, 50, 61, 74, 104, 133, 134, 140, 161, 162, 181, 182, 184, 188, 211, 212, 215
survival, 93, 94, 95, 169, 171, 197
Swami Muktananda, 148
Swami Shivananda, 46
Swami Sivananda, 37
Sydney J. Harris, 116

Z

Other Titles by Bohdi Sanders

Character! Honor! Integrity! Are these traits that guide your life and actions? *Warrior Wisdom: Ageless Wisdom for the Modern Warrior* focuses on how to live your life with character, honor and integrity. This book is highly acclaimed, has won multiple awards and is endorsed by some of the biggest names in martial arts and the world of self-help. *Warrior Wisdom* is filled with wise quotes and useful information for anyone who strives to live a life of excellence. This book will help you live your life to the fullest.

Warrior: The Way of Warriorhood is the second book in the *Warrior Wisdom Series*. Wisdom, life-changing quotes, and entertaining, practical commentaries fill every page. This series has been recognized by four martial arts hall of fame organizations for its inspirational and motivational qualities. The ancient and modern wisdom in this book will definitely help you improve your life and bring meaning to each and every day. The USMAA Hall of Fame awarded Dr. Sanders with Inspiration of the Year for this series!

The Warrior Lifestyle is the last installment of the award winning *Warrior Wisdom Series*. Forwarded by martial arts legend Loren W. Christensen, this book has been dubbed as highly inspirational and motivational. If you want to live your life to the fullest, you need to read this one! Don't settle for an ordinary life, make your life extraordinary! The advice and wisdom shines on every page of this book, making it a must read for everyone who strives to live an extraordinary life of character and honor!

Other Titles by Bohdi Sanders

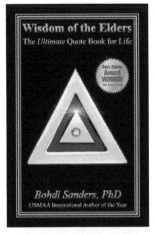

Wisdom of the Elders is a unique, one-of-a-kind quote book. This book is filled with quotes that focus on living life to the fullest with honor, character, and integrity. Honored by the USA Book News with a 1st place award for Best Books of the Year in 2010, this book is a guide for life. *Wisdom of the Elders* contains over 4,800 quotes, all which lead the reader to a life of excellence. If you enjoy quotes, wisdom, and knowledge, you will love this book. This is truly the ultimate quote book for those searching for wisdom!

Defensive Living takes the reader deep into the minds of nine of the most revered masters of worldly wisdom. It reveals valuable insights concerning human nature from some of the greatest minds the world has ever known, such as Sun Tzu, Gracian, Goethe, and others. *Defensive Living* presents invaluable lessons for living and advice for avoiding the many pitfalls of human relationships. This is an invaluable and entertaining guidebook for living a successful and rewarding life!

Secrets of the Soul is a guide to uncovering your deeply hidden beliefs. This delightful book provides over 1,150 probing questions which guide you to a thorough understanding of who you are and what you believe. Take this unbelievably entertaining journey to a much deeper place of self-awareness. Where do your beliefs come from? Do you really know exactly what you believe and why you believe it? You will after reading *Secrets of the Soul*. This book will help you uncover your true beliefs!

Looking for More Wisdom?

If you are interested in living the warrior lifestyle or simply in living a life of character, integrity and honor you will enjoy The Wisdom Warrior website and newsletter. The Wisdom Warrior website contains dozens of articles, useful links, and news for those seeking to live the warrior lifestyle.

The newsletter is also a valuable resource. Each edition of The Wisdom Warrior Newsletter is packed with motivating quotes, articles, and information which everyone will find useful in their journey to perfect their character and live the life which they were meant to live.

The Wisdom Warrior Newsletter is a newsletter sent directly to your email account and is absolutely FREE! There is no cost or obligation to you whatsoever. You will also receive the current news updates and new articles by Dr. Bohdi Sanders as soon as they are available. Your email address is never shared with anyone else.

All you need to do to start receiving this valuable and informative newsletter is to go to the Wisdom Warrior website and simply sign up. It is that simple! You will find The Wisdom Warrior website at:

www.TheWisdomWarrior.com

Also, be sure to find posts by Dr. Sanders on Facebook. Dr. Sanders posts enlightening commentaries, photographs, and quotes throughout the week on his Facebook pages. You can find them at:

www.facebook.com/The.Warrior.Lifestyle

www.facebook.com/EldersWisdom

www.facebook.com/bohdi.sanders

Don't miss the opportunity to receive tons of FREE wisdom, enlightening posts, interesting articles, and intriguing photographs on The Wisdom Warrior website and on Dr. Sanders' Facebook pages.

Sign Up Today!

Martial Arts Honors
for Dr. Sanders' Books

Dr. Sanders' books have been honored by the follow organizations for
their significant contributions to the world of martial arts: